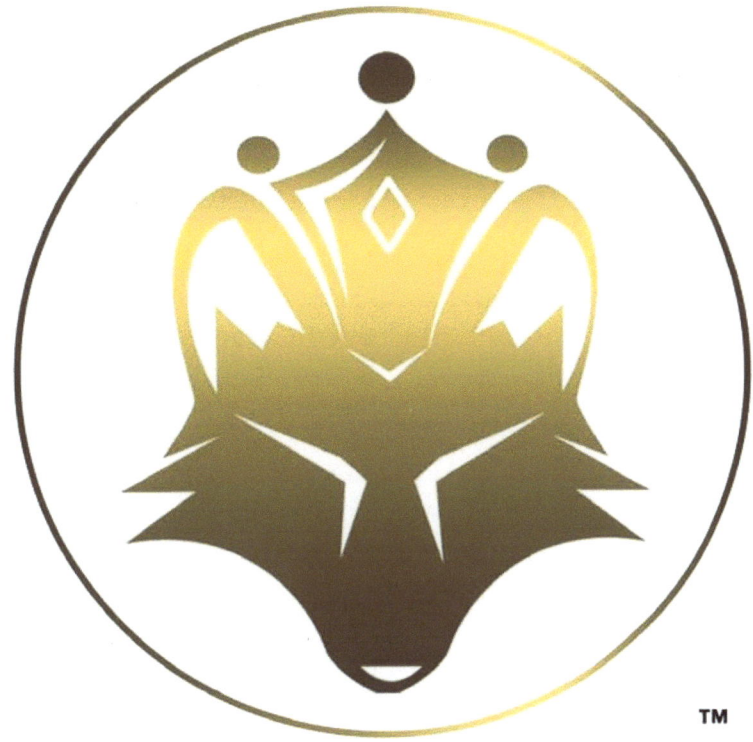

The Gold Standard for Gentlemen Entertainment

WWW.FOXTAILMAG.COM

FOXTAIL Magazine (ISSN #978-1979-659352), Issue #10 (RE-Release, November 2017), is published bi-monthly by **Foxtail, Inc.**, 945 W. Agatite Ave., Chicago, IL 60640. The subscription rate is $24.95 per year. One-year subscriptions rates: U.S., $24.95; Canada, $54.95; for all other countries, $84.95 in prepaid U.S. funds. Periodicals postage paid at Chicago, IL and additional mailing offices. POSTMASTER: Send address changes to *FOXTAIL Magazine,* 945 W. Agatite Ave., Chicago, IL 60640,. Reproduction or use of any part of Issue #20 (October 2016) of *FOXTAIL* without the written consent of the publisher is prohibited. Return postage must accompany all manuscripts, drawings or photographs. All manuscripts, drawings or photographs sent to *FOXTAIL* will be treated as unconditionally assigned for publication and copyright purposes and are subject to the magazine's right to edit and comment editorially. *FOXTAIL* assumes no responsibility for the advertisements made herein or the quality and availability of the products advertised herein. *FOXTAIL* assumes no responsibility to determine whether the people whose photographs or statements appear in such advertisements have, in fact, endorsed such products or consented to the use of their names or photographs, or the statements attributed to them. The publisher is exempt from the record-keeping requirements and disclosure statements mandated by 18 U.S. Code, Section 2257 A - C and the pertinent regulations, 28 C.F.R. Ch.1, Part 75, since all of such material falls within the exempted material set forth in Section 75(a) (1-3) of the regulations.

For Advertising Information Contact:
Foxtail Magazine
945 W. Agatite Ave.
Chicago, IL 60640-4044
advertising@foxtailmag.com

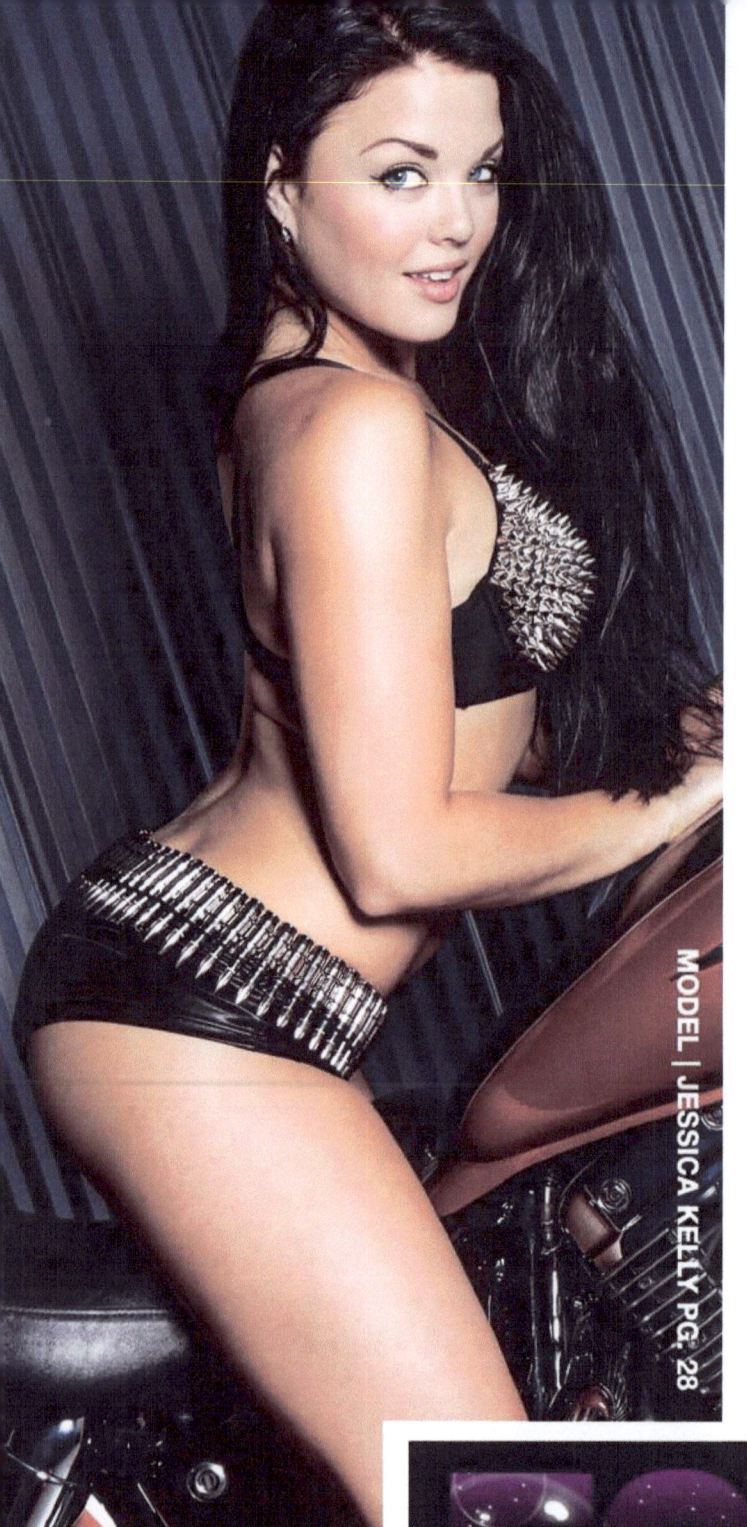

MODEL | JESSICA KELLY PG. 28

FOXTAIL MAGAZINE
BEAUTY IS LIFE, AND LIFE IS BEAUTIFUL

EDITOR-IN-CHIEF
Charles C. Rigby II
charles.rigby@foxtailmag.com

SENIOR EDITOR
Tony Rudd
tony.rudd@foxtailmag.com

SENIOR PHOTOGRAPHY
Sinovah Kane
sinovakane@gmail.com

GRAPHIC DESIGN/PHOTO EDITING
Sinovah Kane Studios
sinovakane@gmail.com

CONTRIBUTING PHOTOGRAPHERS
Greater Images Photos
Sinovah Kane Studios
Nick Weaver
Murder City Angels
Dan Nakon Photography
Nando Pro Photography
LRS Photography
Beauty Boots Modeling Agency
Daniel FX

CONTACT
info@foxtailmag.com
modeling@foxtailmag.com
submissions@foxtailmag.com

ADVERTISING
advertising@foxtailmag.com

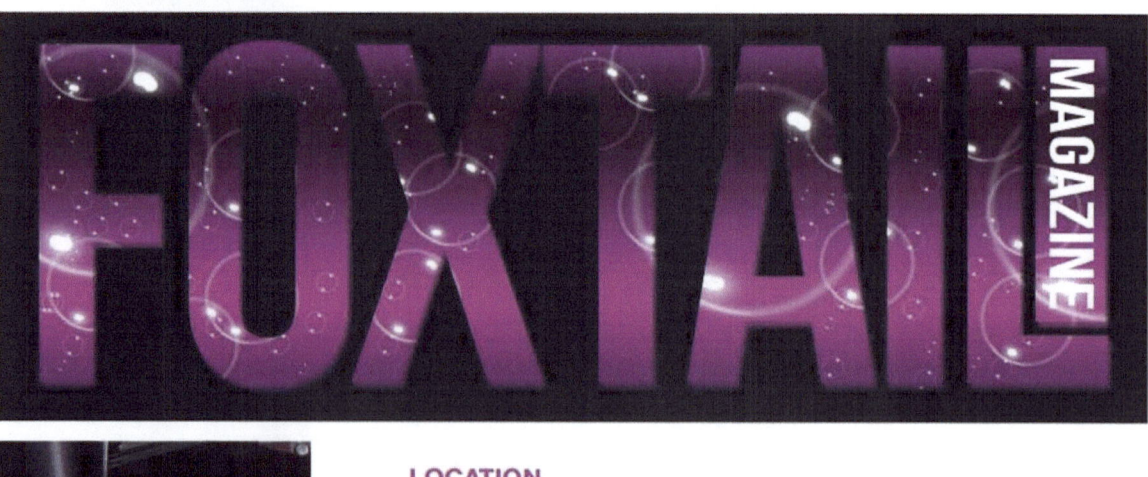

LOCATION
1245 South Michigan Ave., Suite 115, Chicago, IL 60605

WWW.FOXTAILMAG.COM

FOXTAIL MAGAZINE

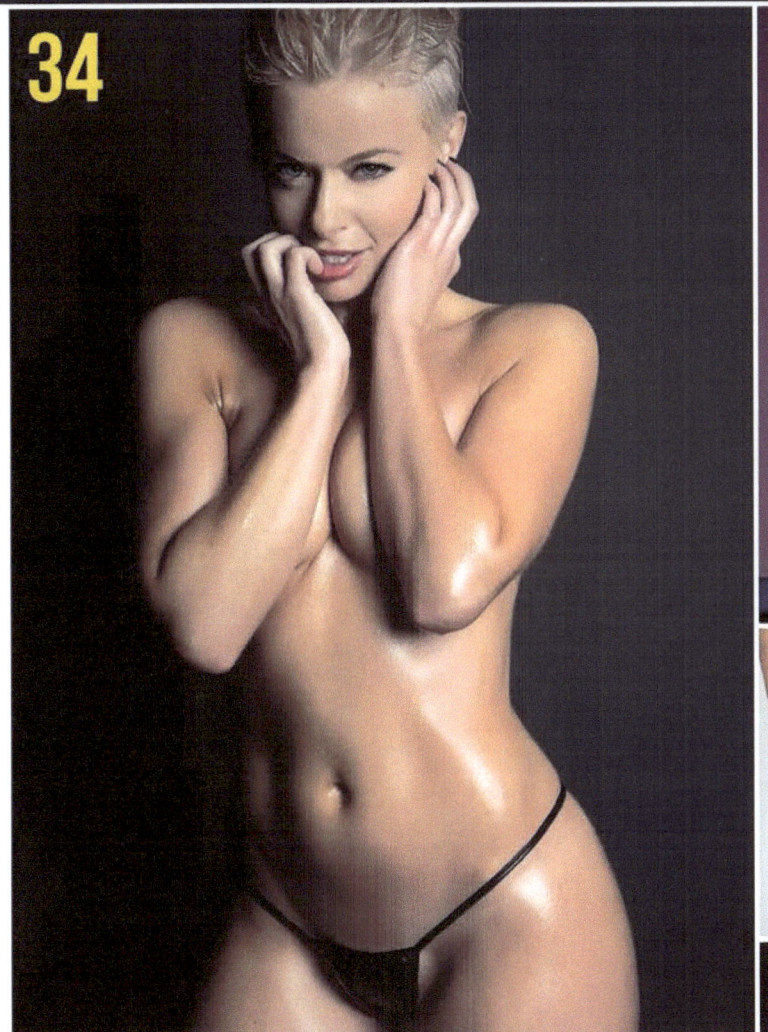
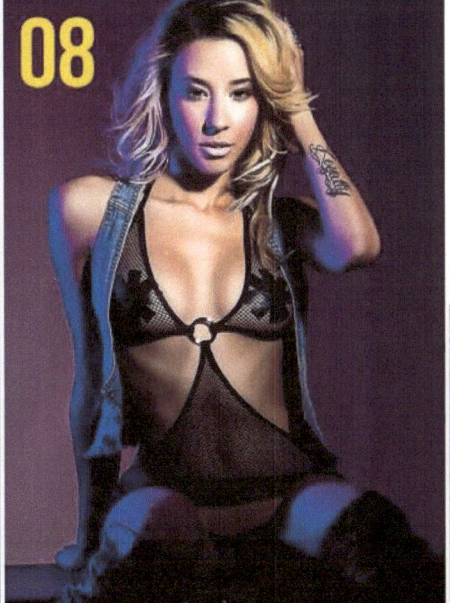
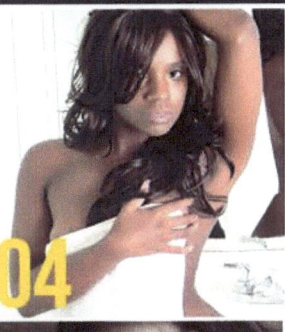
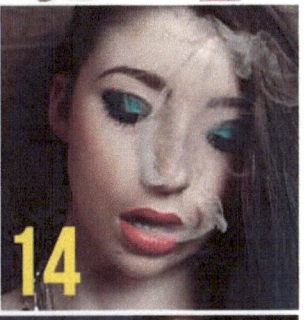
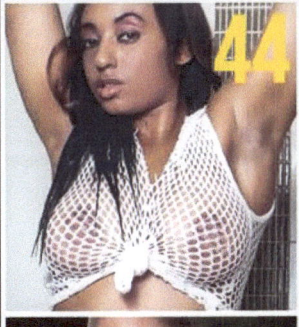
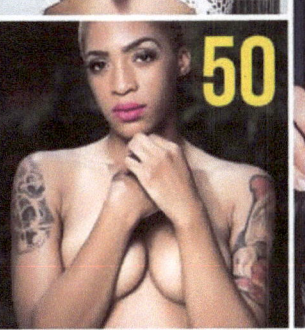
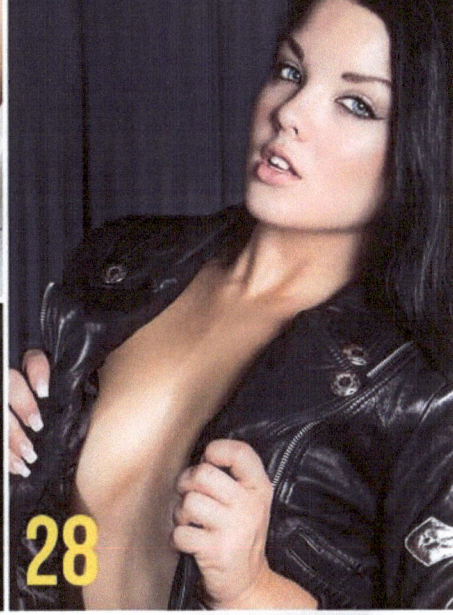
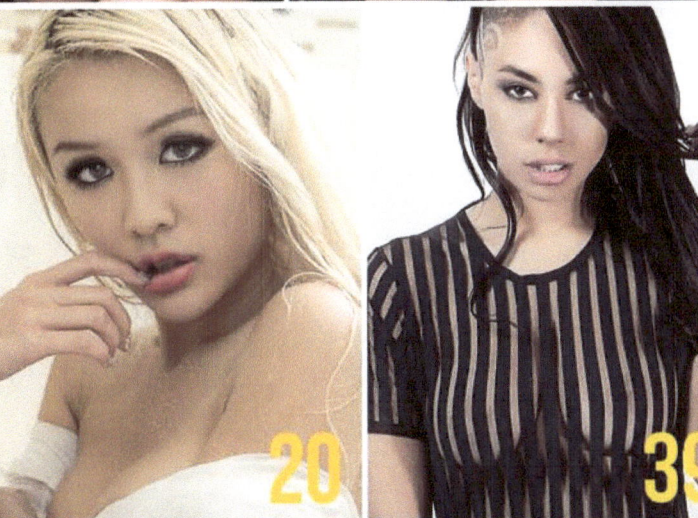

IN THIS ISSUE OF FOXTAIL

CHOCOLATE PUDDING	04
CHINA NABY	08
BRENNA MURPHY	14
CHELLEY L.	20
JESSICA KELLY	28
LILY MARIE	34
JASMENE NICOLE	39
SUMMER MONROE	44
OBSESSION	52

OUR SEXIEST ISSUE YET!
#FOXTAILGIRLS

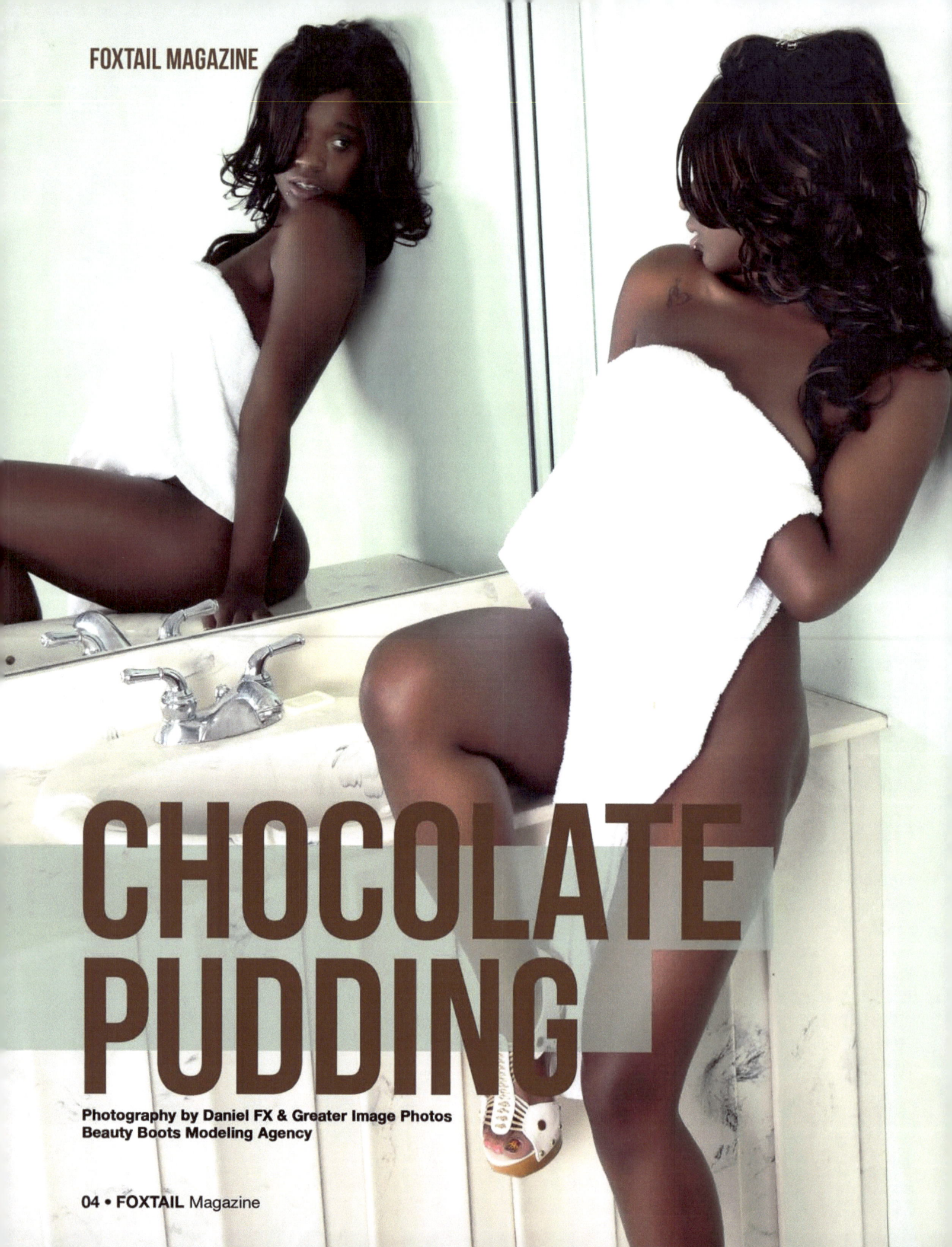

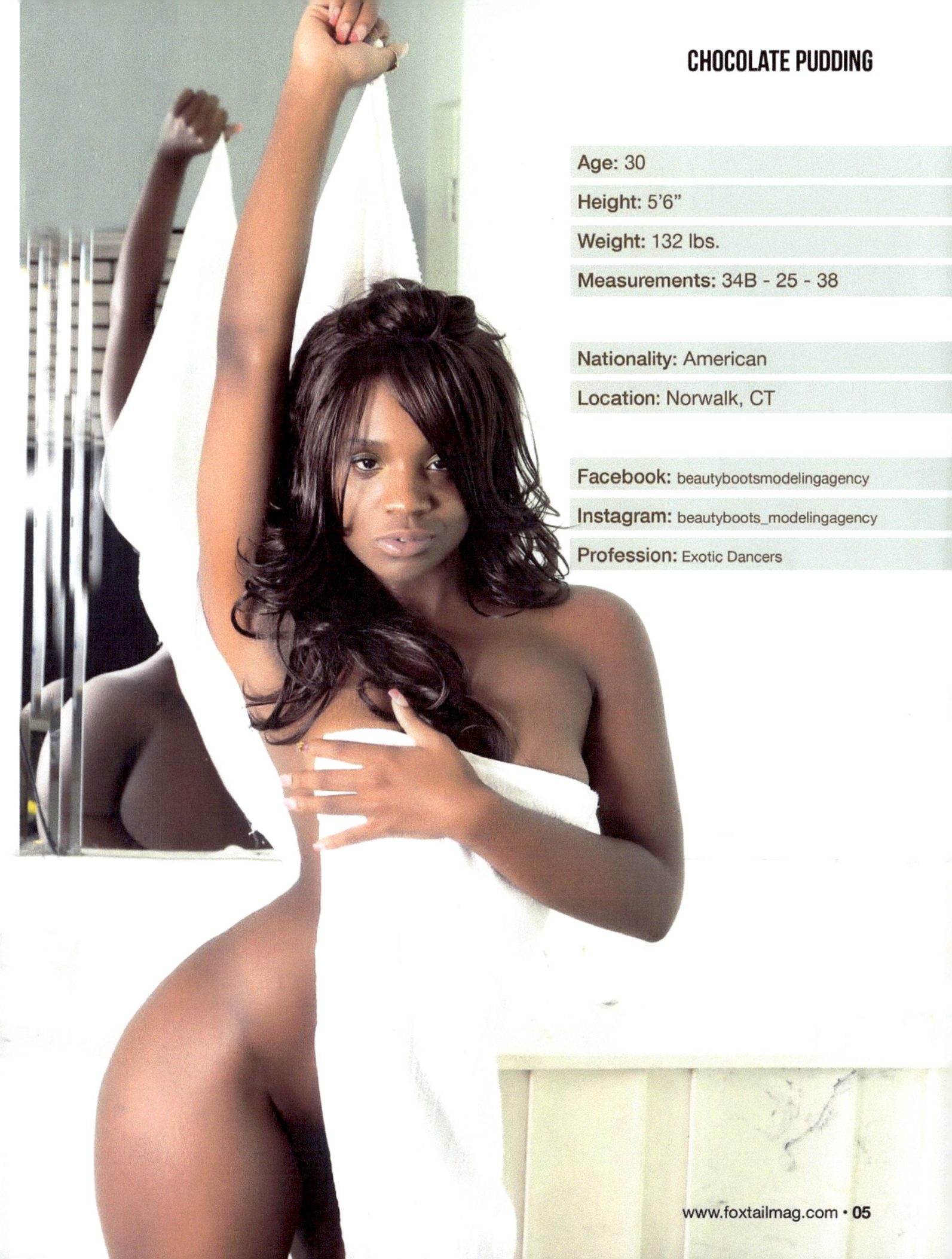

CHOCOLATE PUDDING

Age: 30

Height: 5'6"

Weight: 132 lbs.

Measurements: 34B - 25 - 38

Nationality: American

Location: Norwalk, CT

Facebook: beautybootsmodelingagency

Instagram: beautyboots_modelingagency

Profession: Exotic Dancers

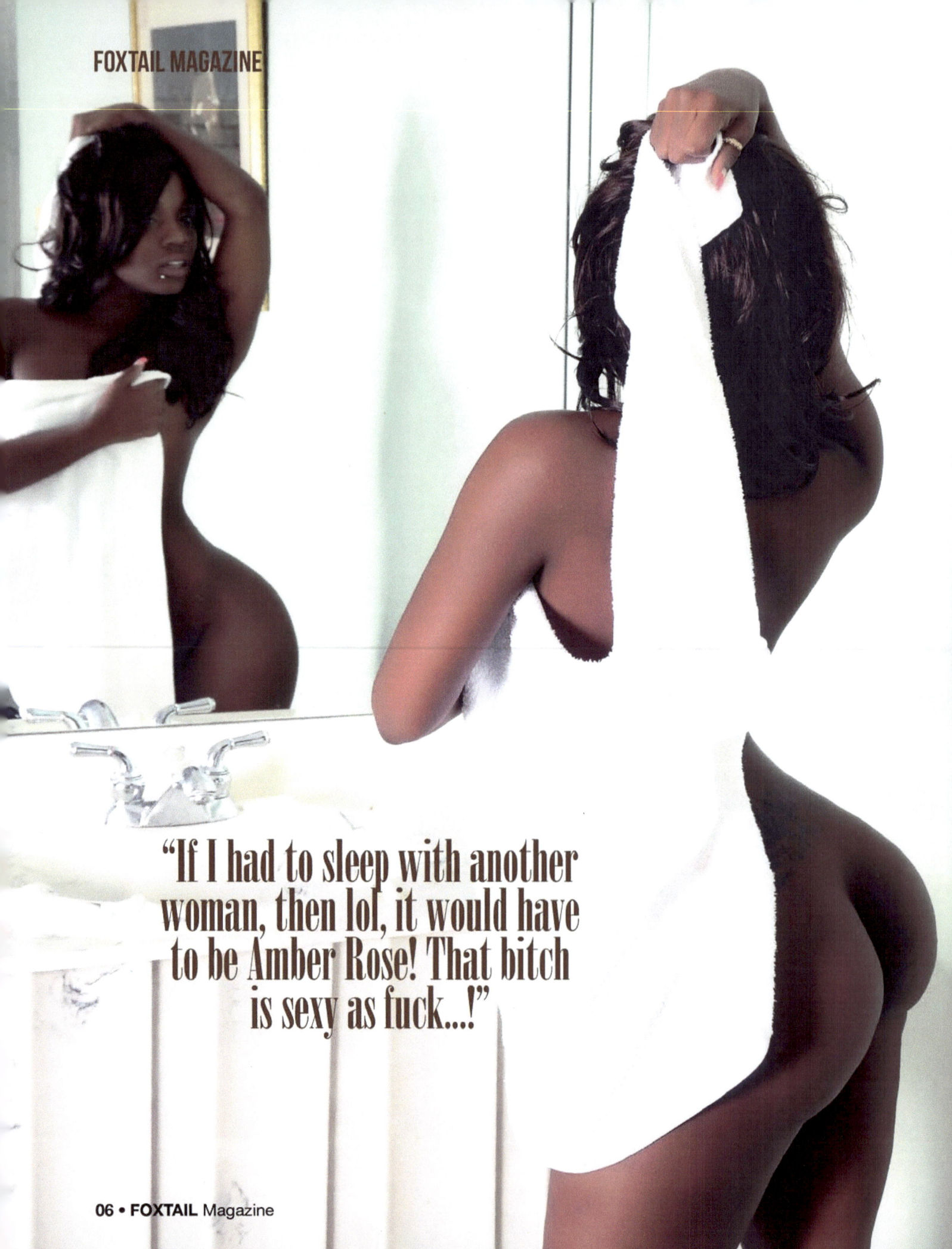

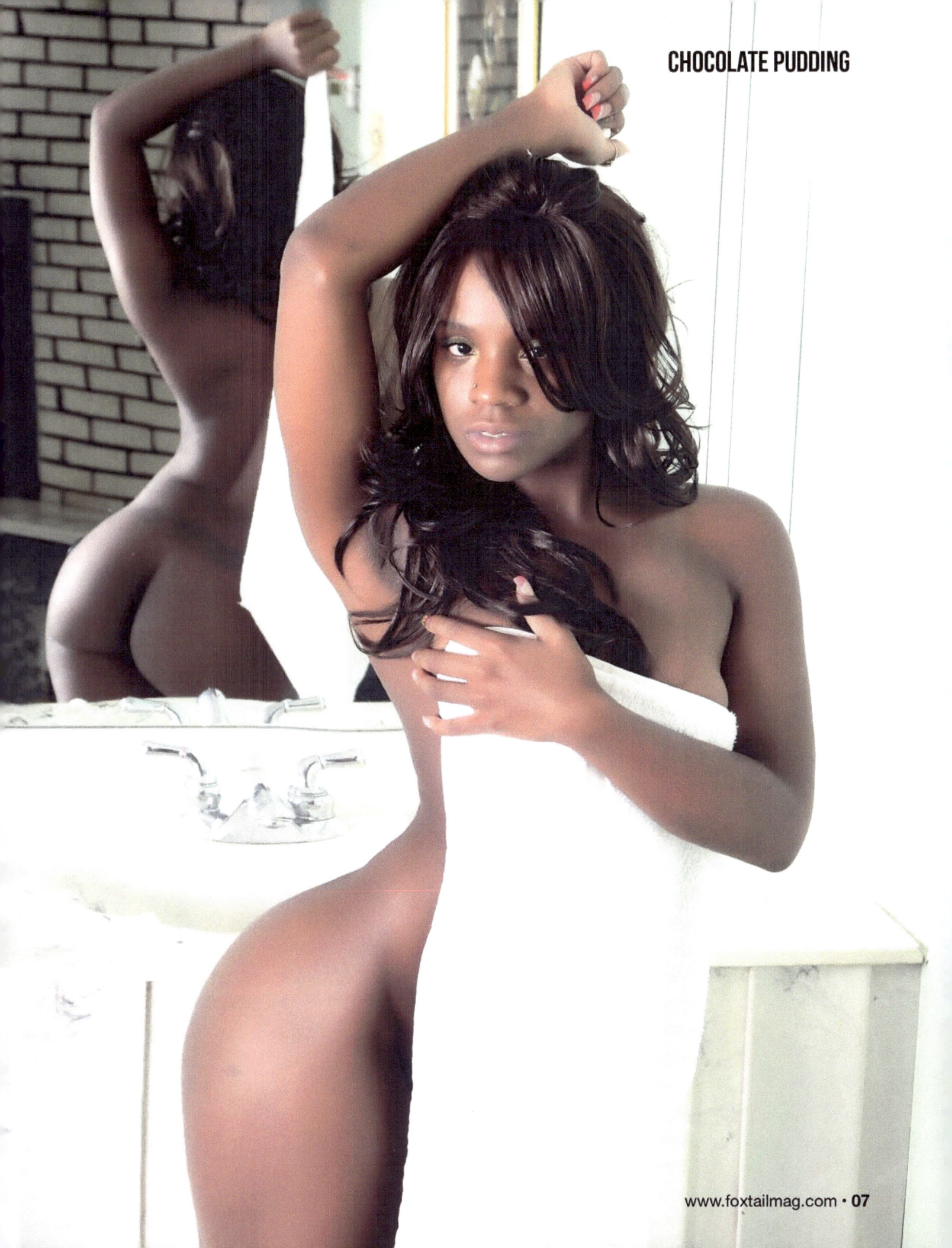

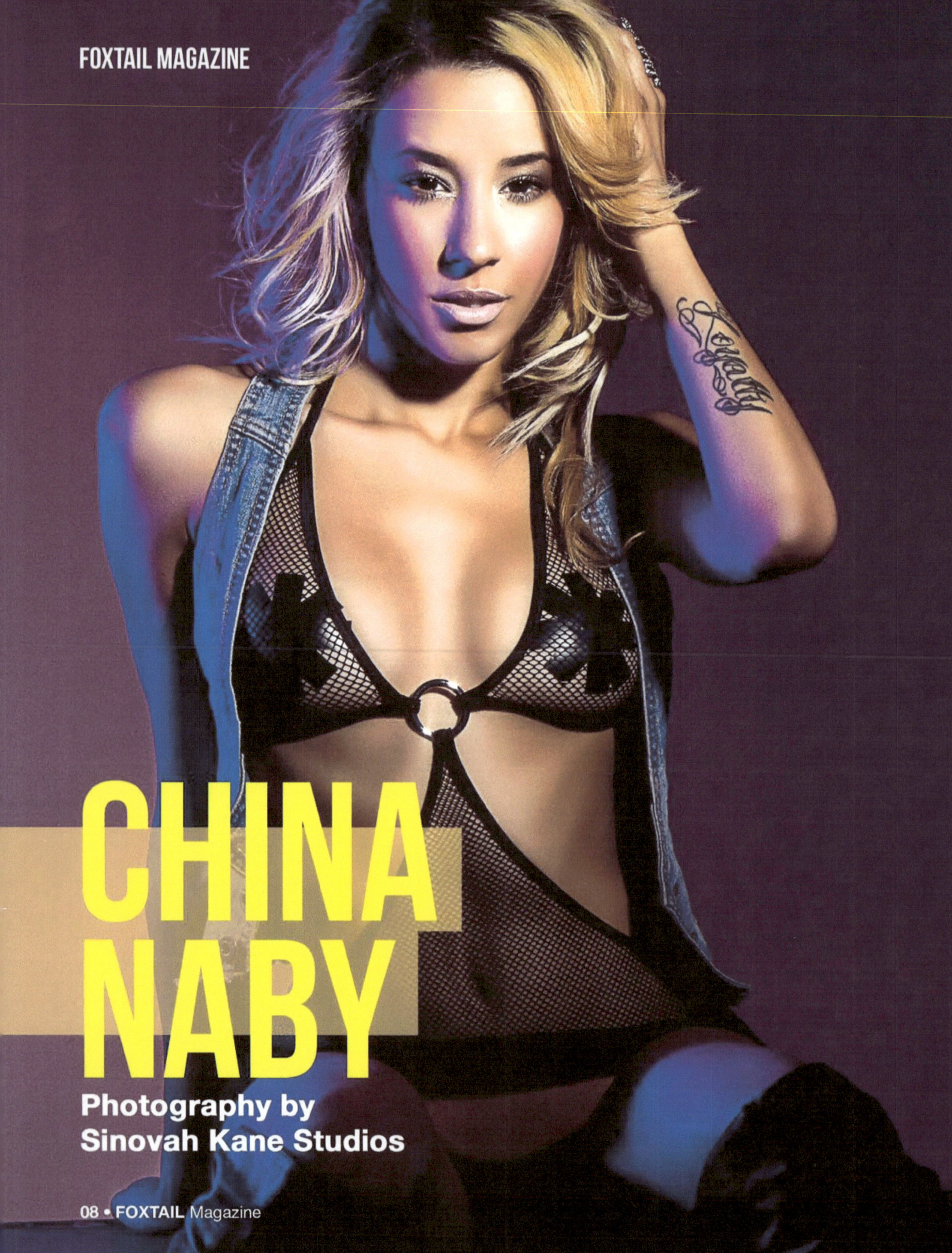

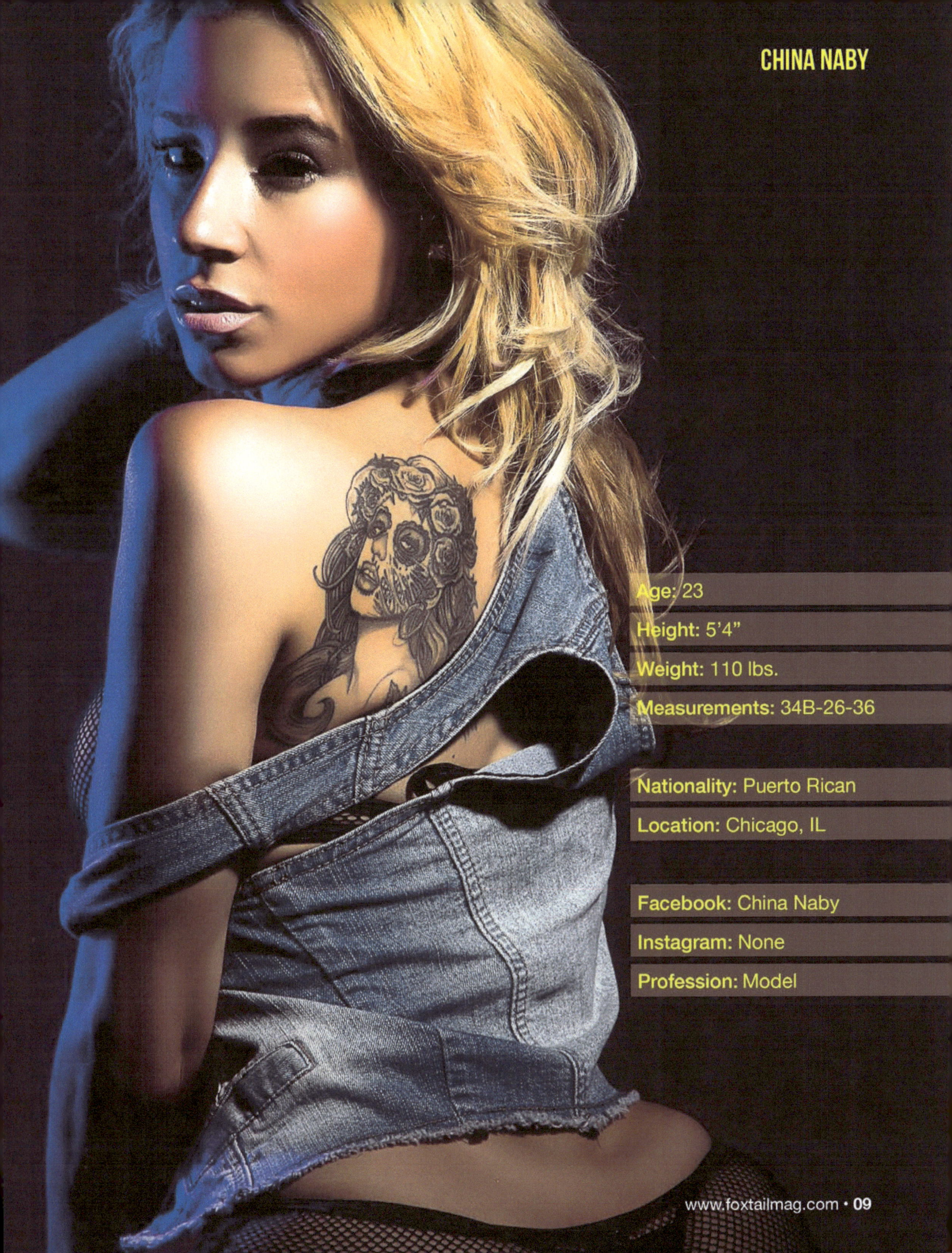

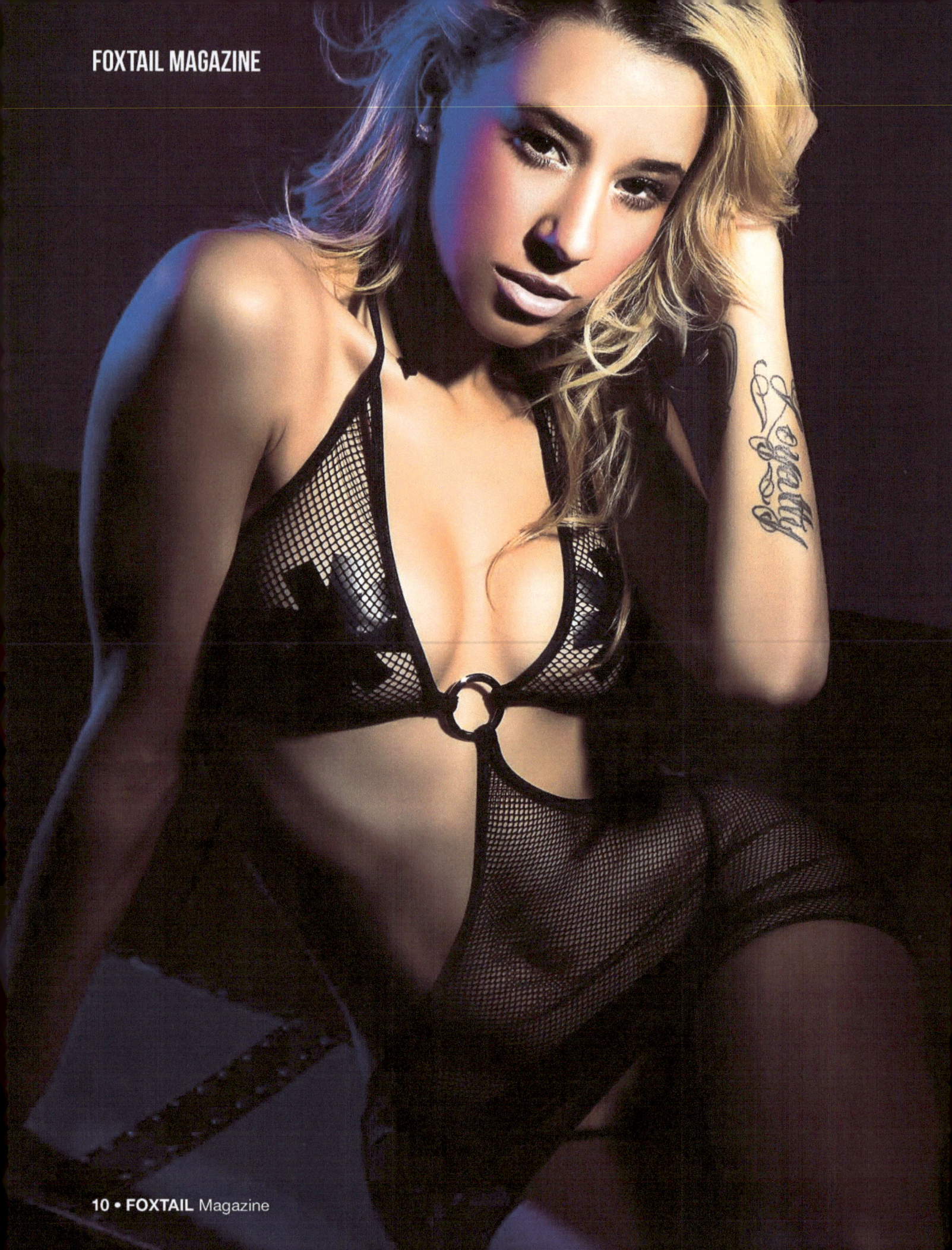

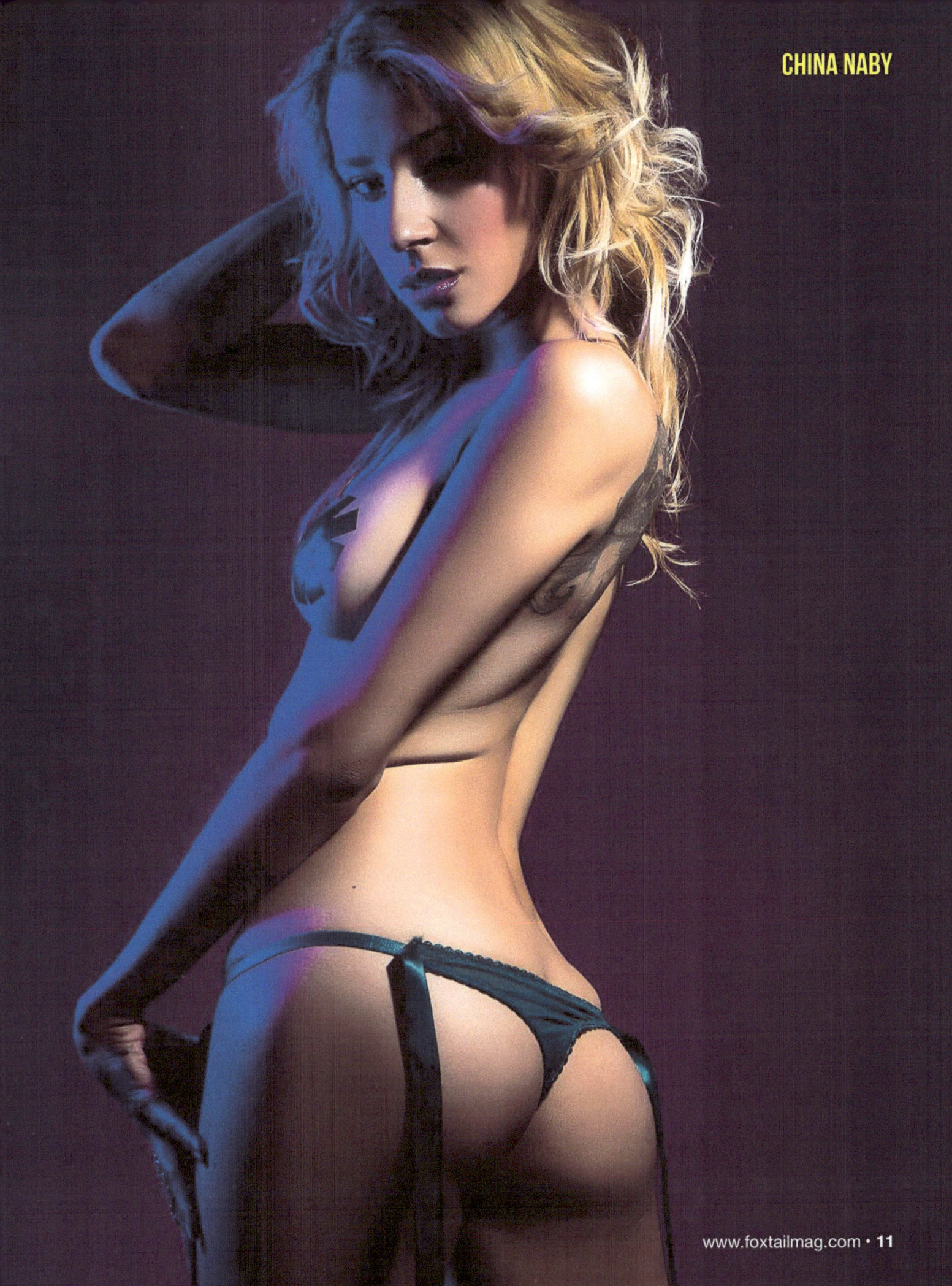

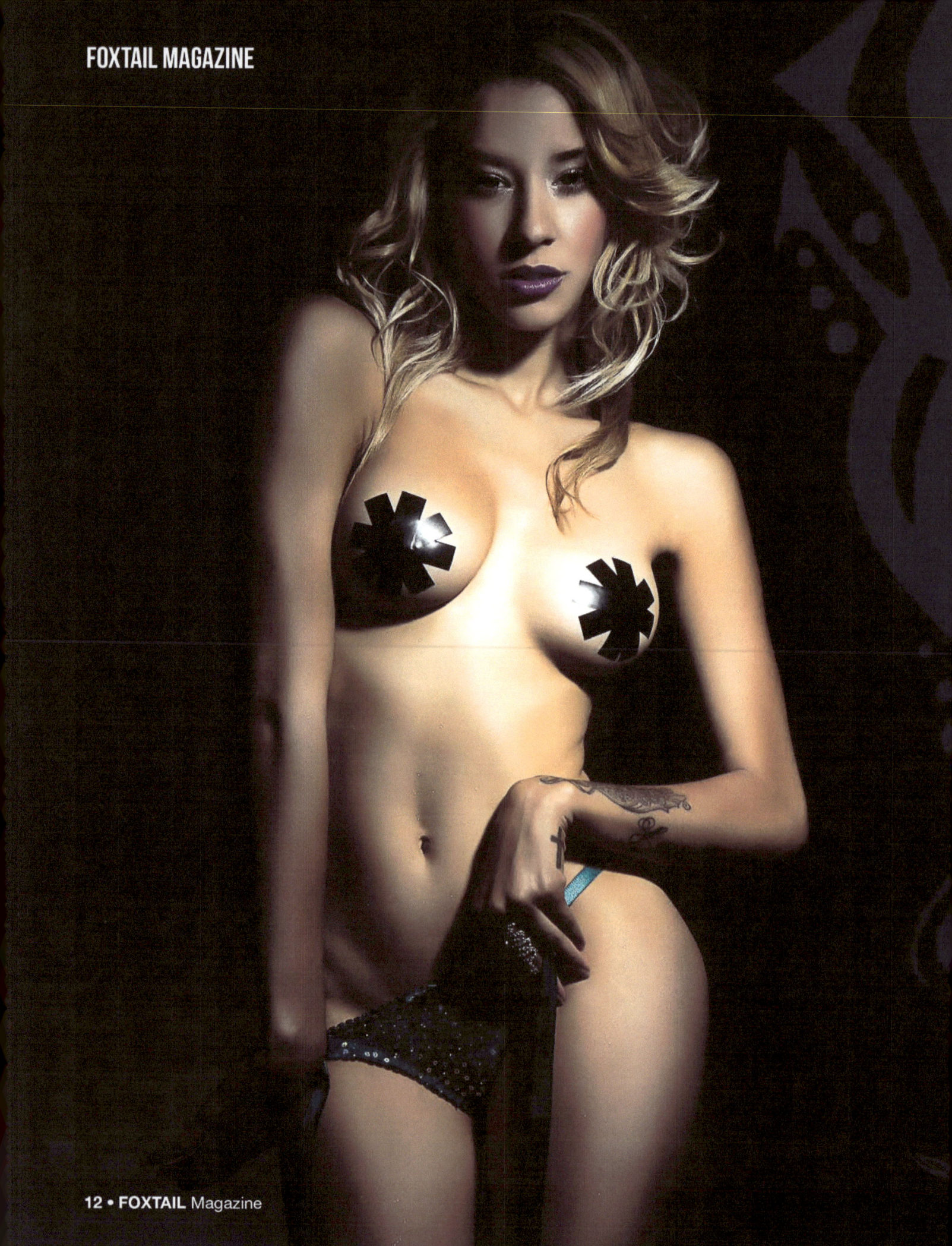

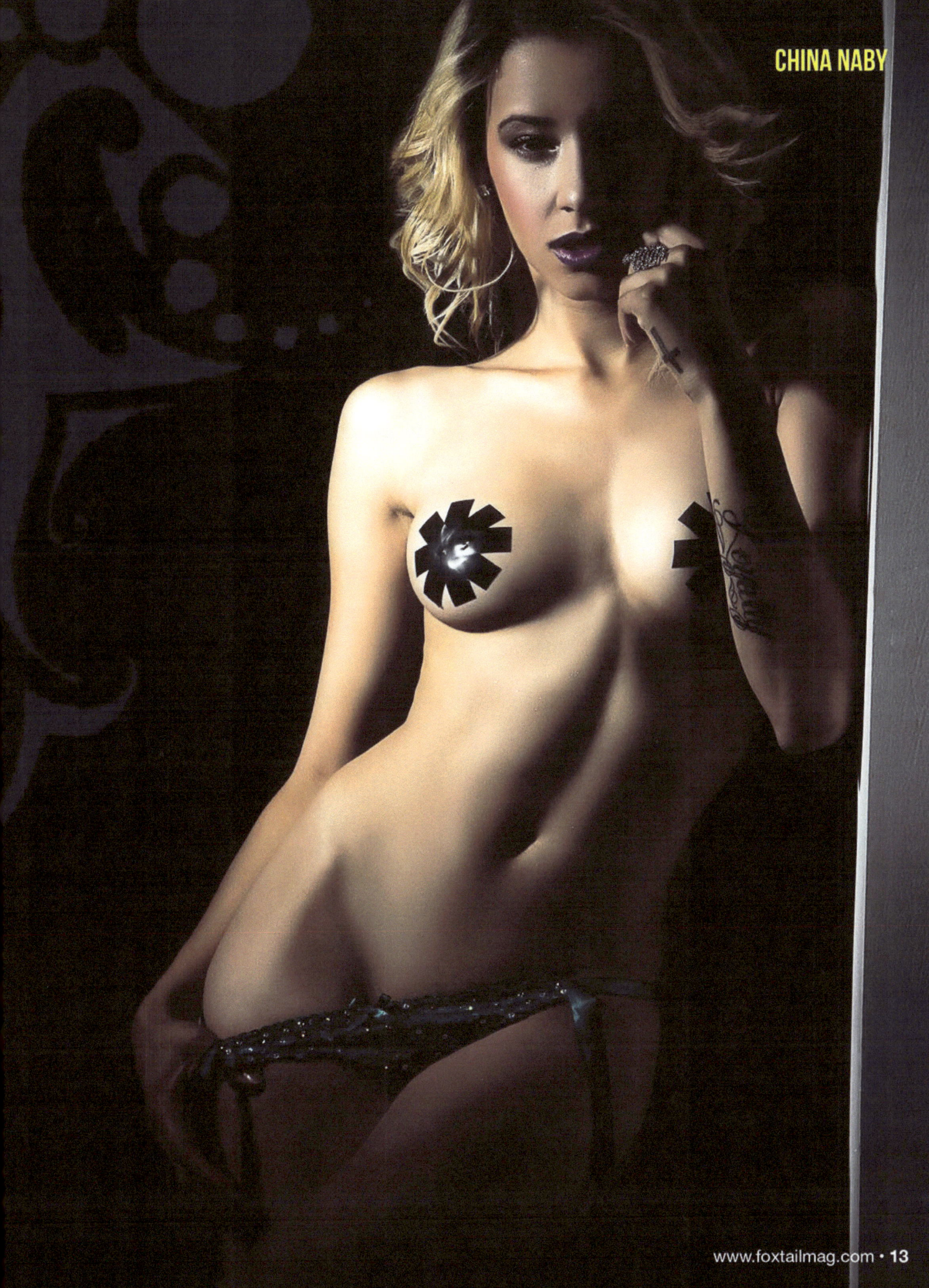

BRENNA MURPHY

Photography by Nick Weaver

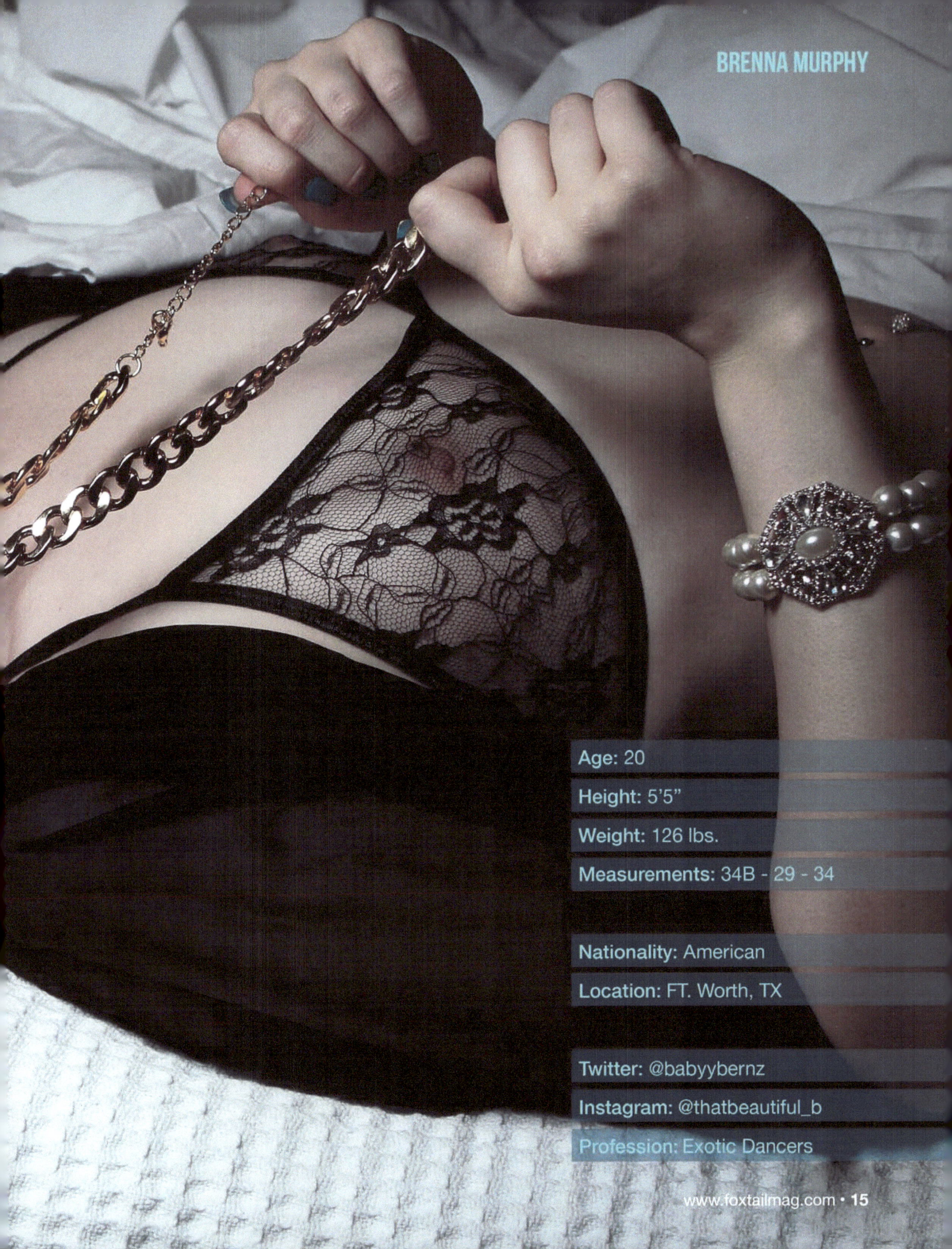

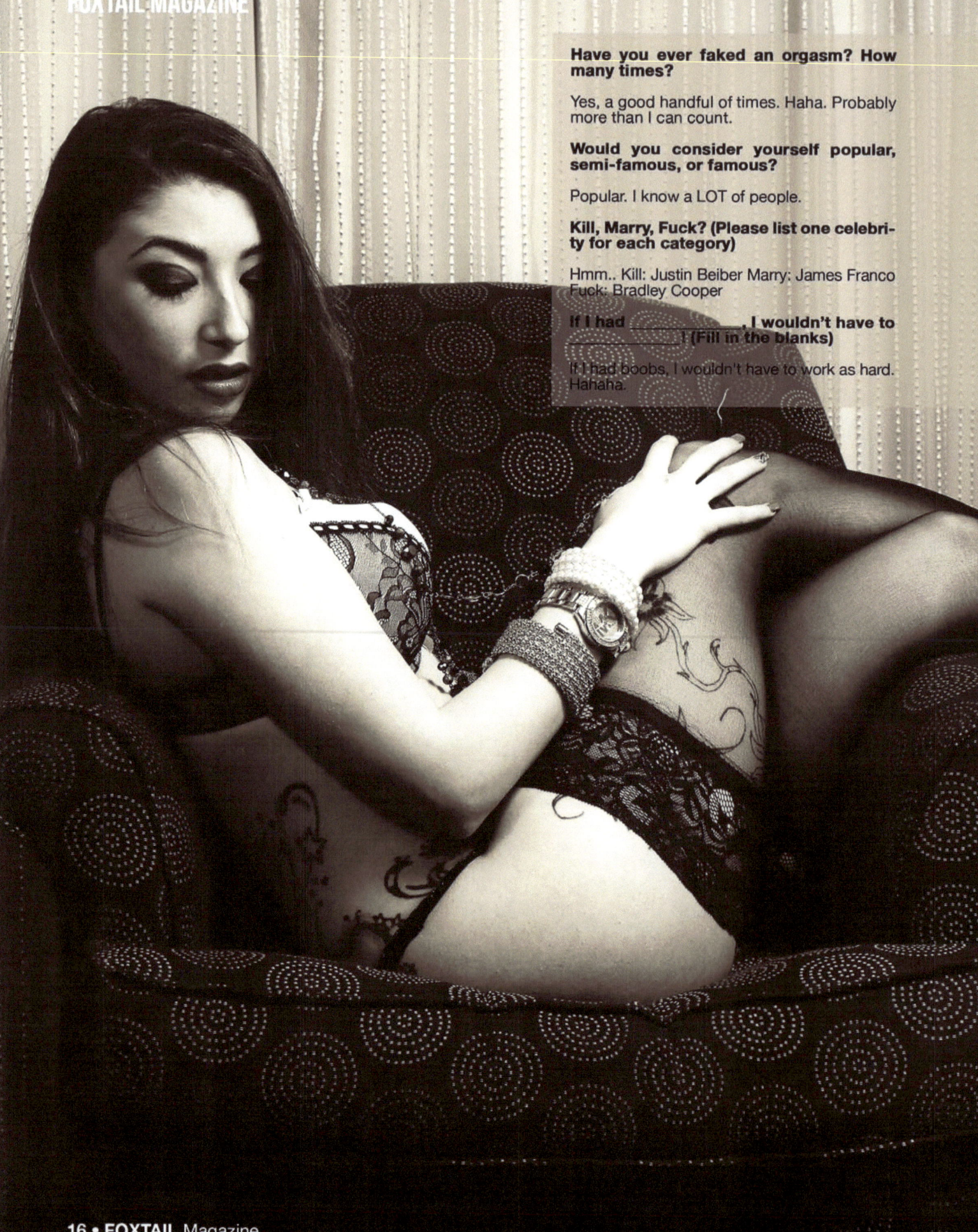

Have you ever faked an orgasm? How many times?

Yes, a good handful of times. Haha. Probably more than I can count.

Would you consider yourself popular, semi-famous, or famous?

Popular. I know a LOT of people.

Kill, Marry, Fuck? (Please list one celebrity for each category)

Hmm.. Kill: Justin Beiber Marry: James Franco Fuck: Bradley Cooper

If I had _____, I wouldn't have to _____! (Fill in the blanks)

If I had boobs, I wouldn't have to work as hard. Hahaha.

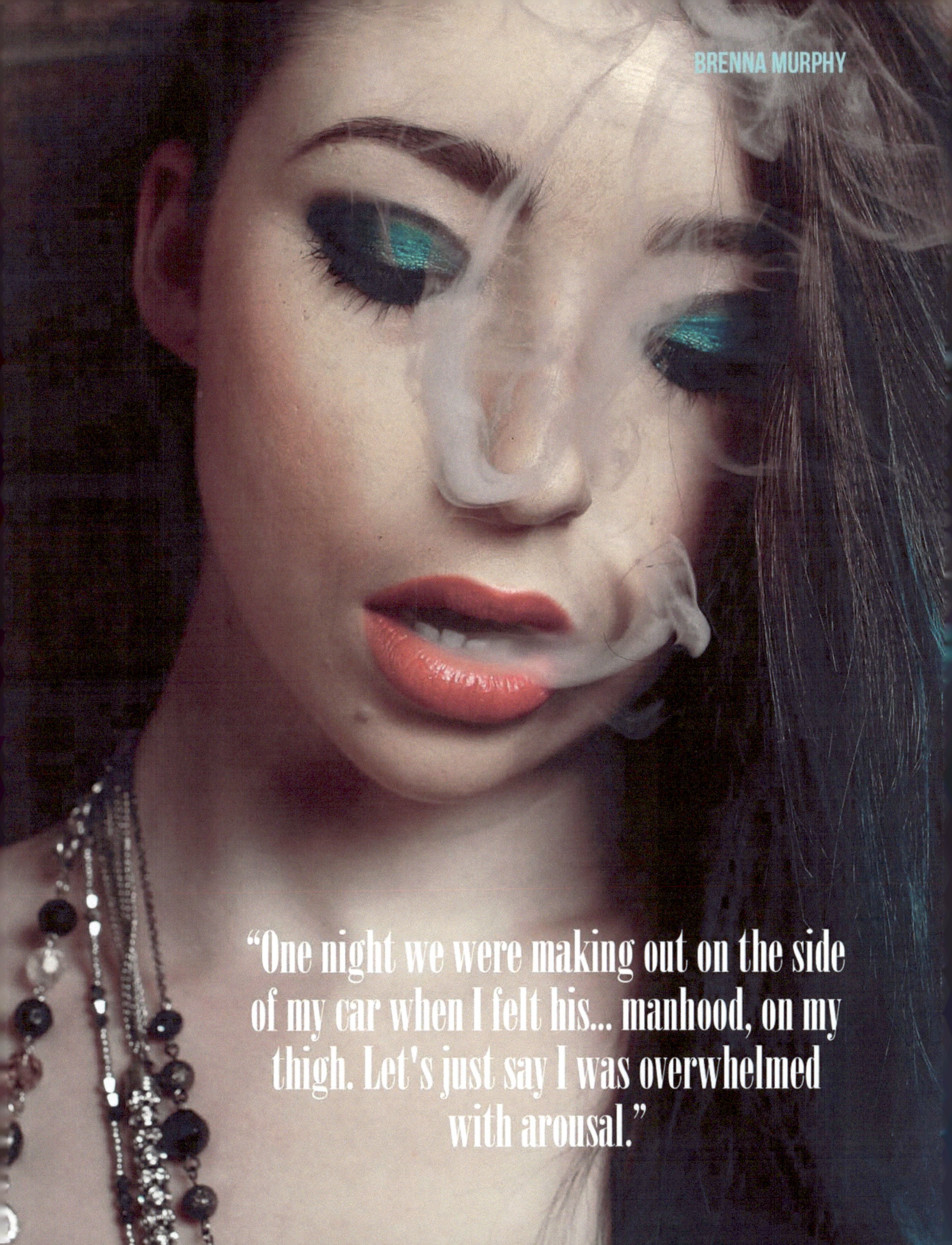

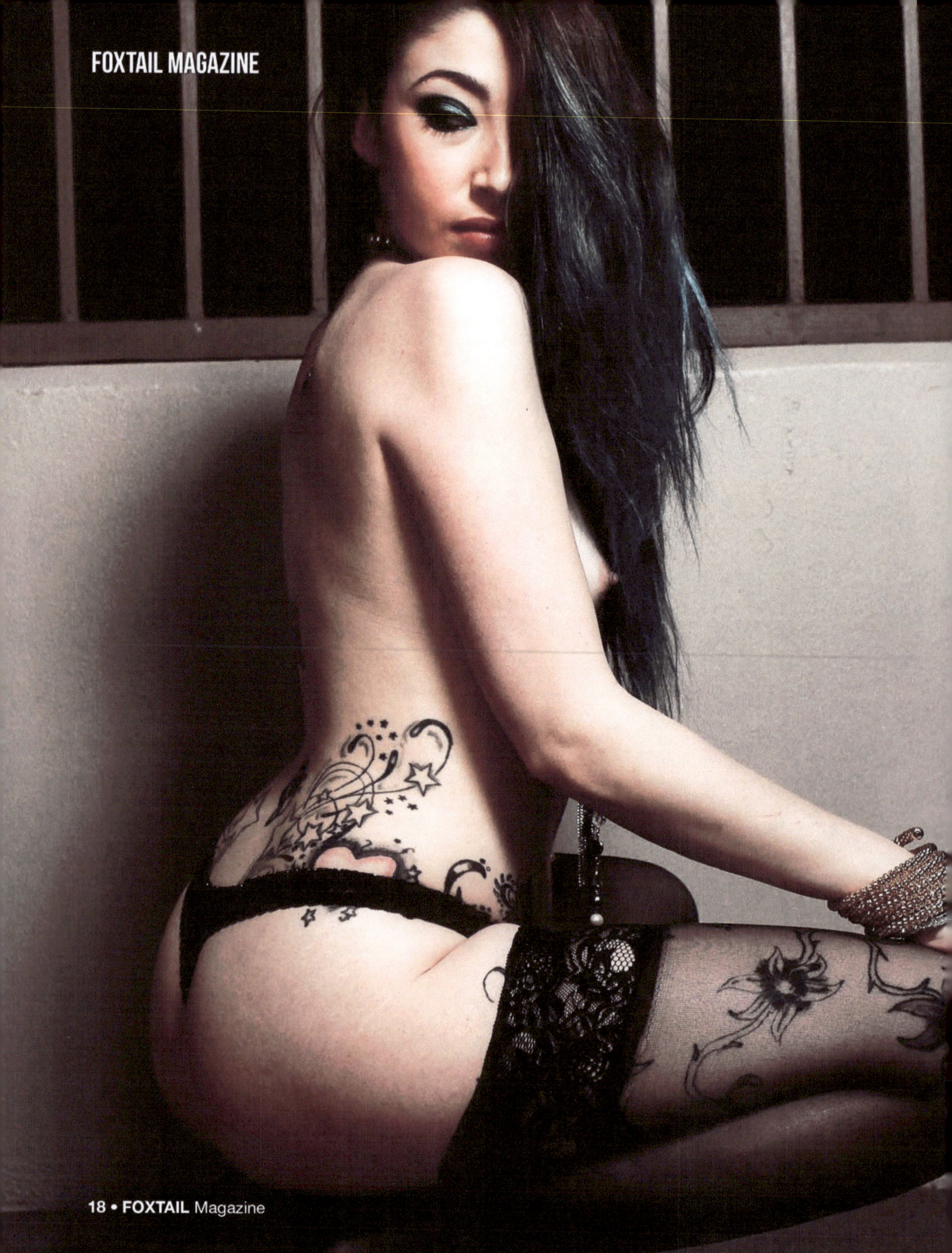

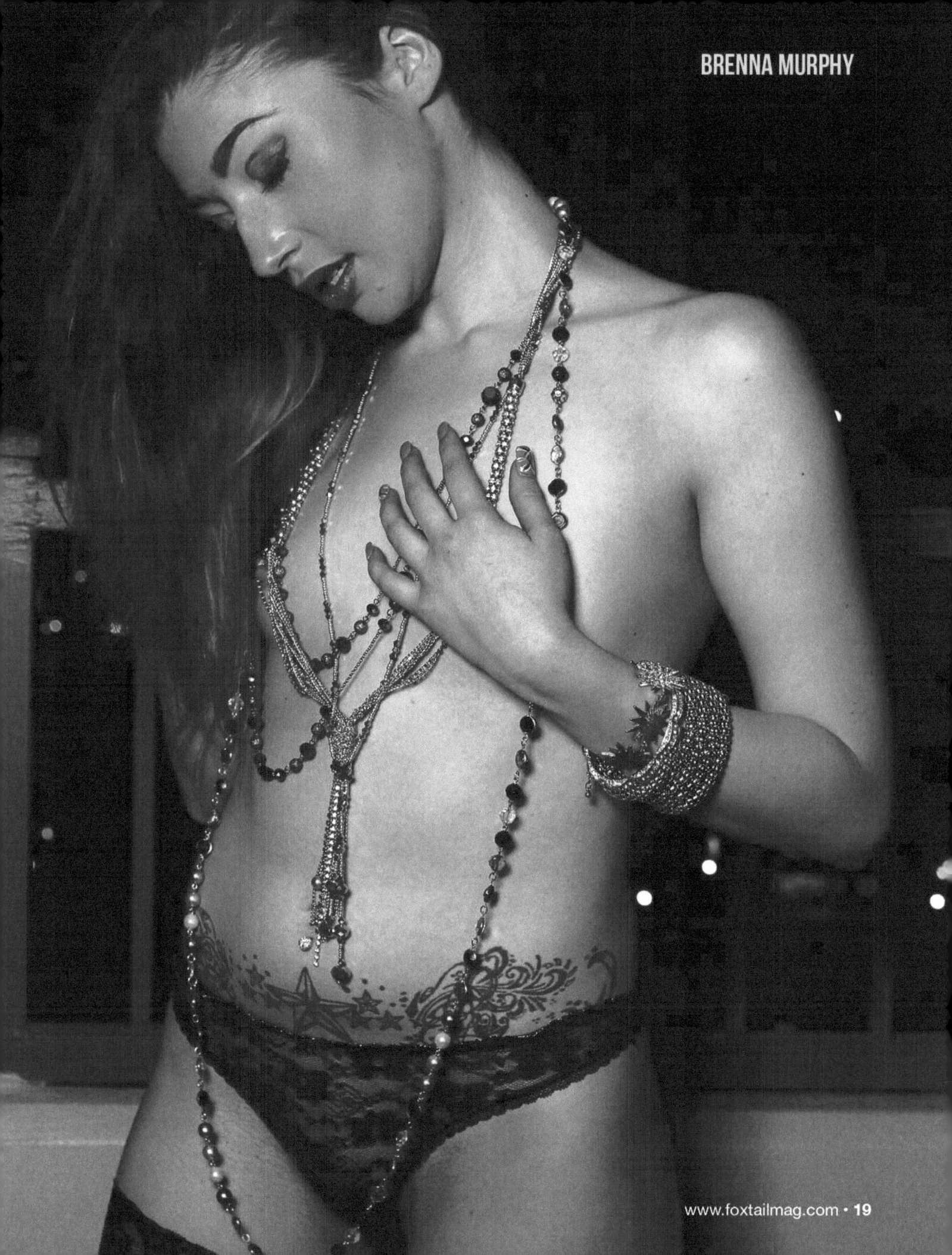

FOXTAIL MAGAZINE | FOX CANDY GIRL OF THE MONTH

CHELLEY L.

Photography by Dan Nakon

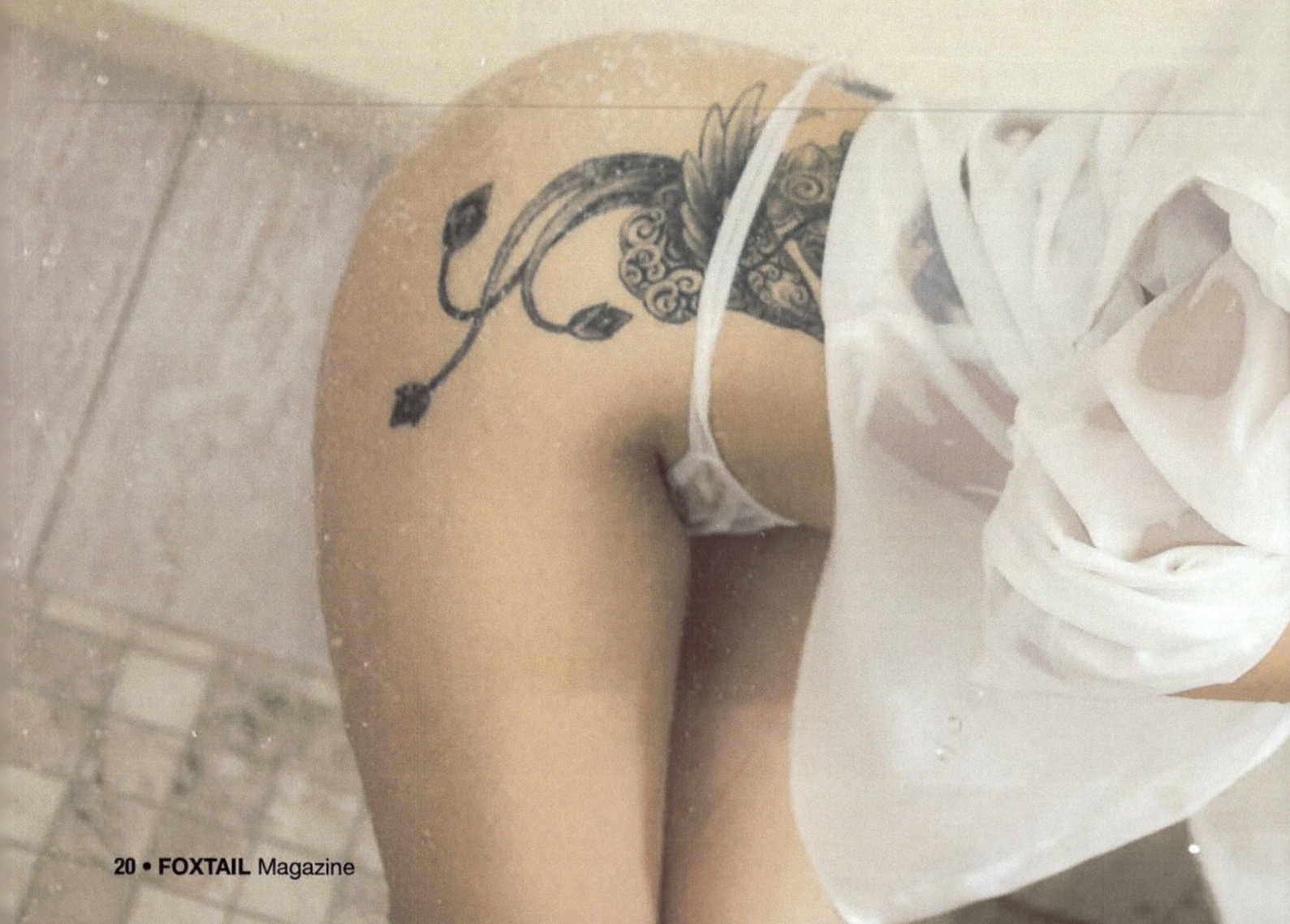

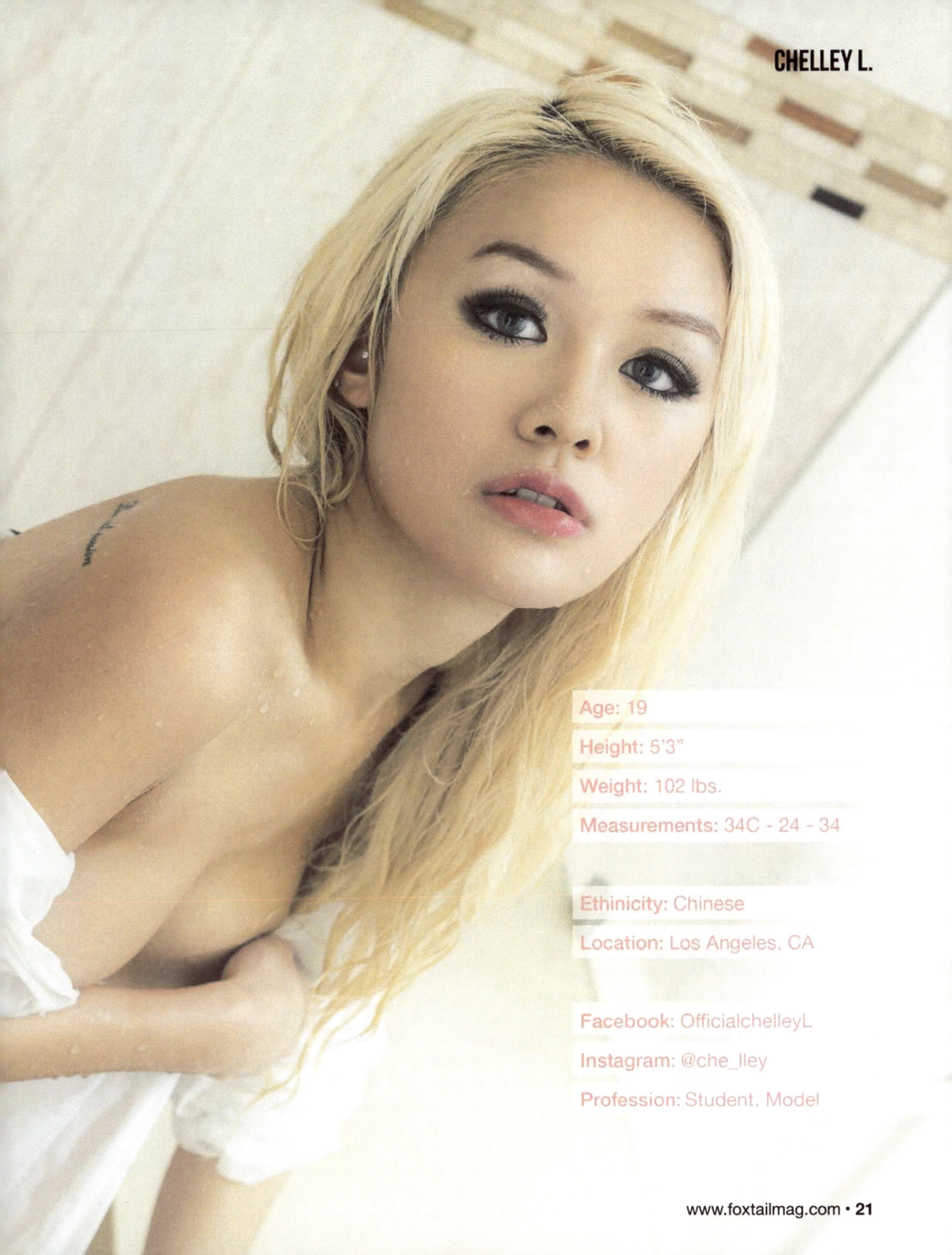

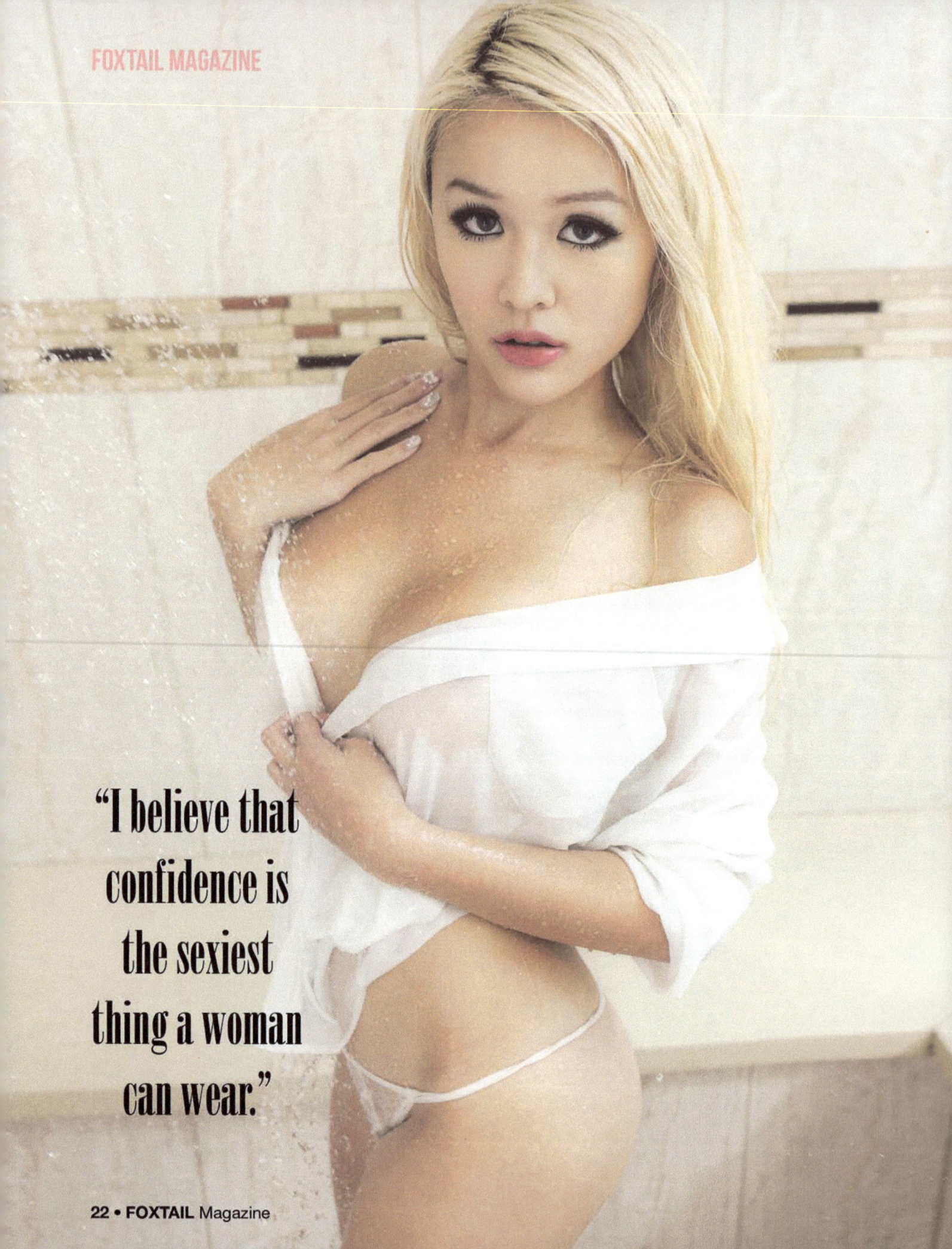

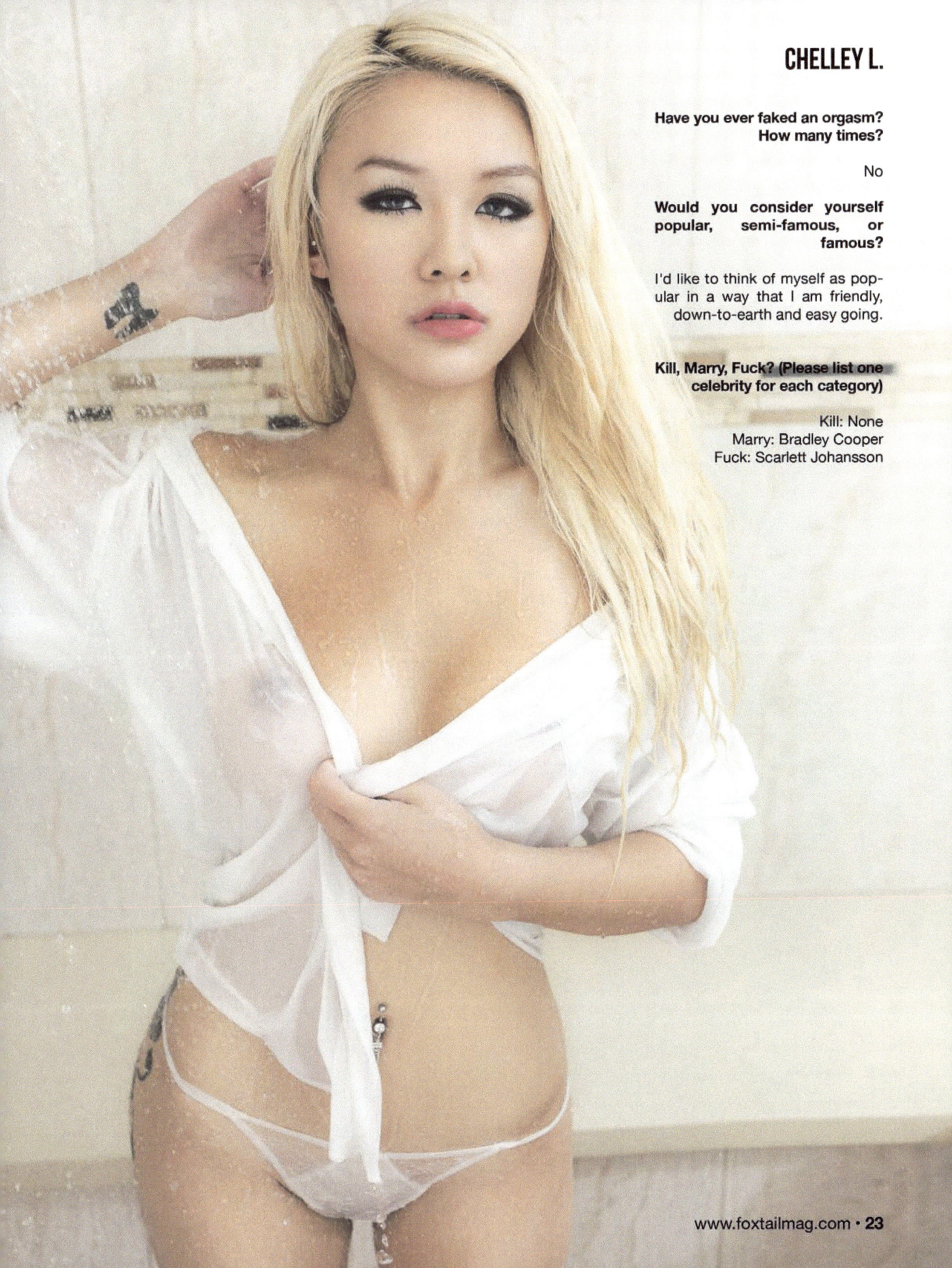

CHELLEY L.

Have you ever faked an orgasm? How many times?

No

Would you consider yourself popular, semi-famous, or famous?

I'd like to think of myself as popular in a way that I am friendly, down-to-earth and easy going.

Kill, Marry, Fuck? (Please list one celebrity for each category)

Kill: None
Marry: Bradley Cooper
Fuck: Scarlett Johansson

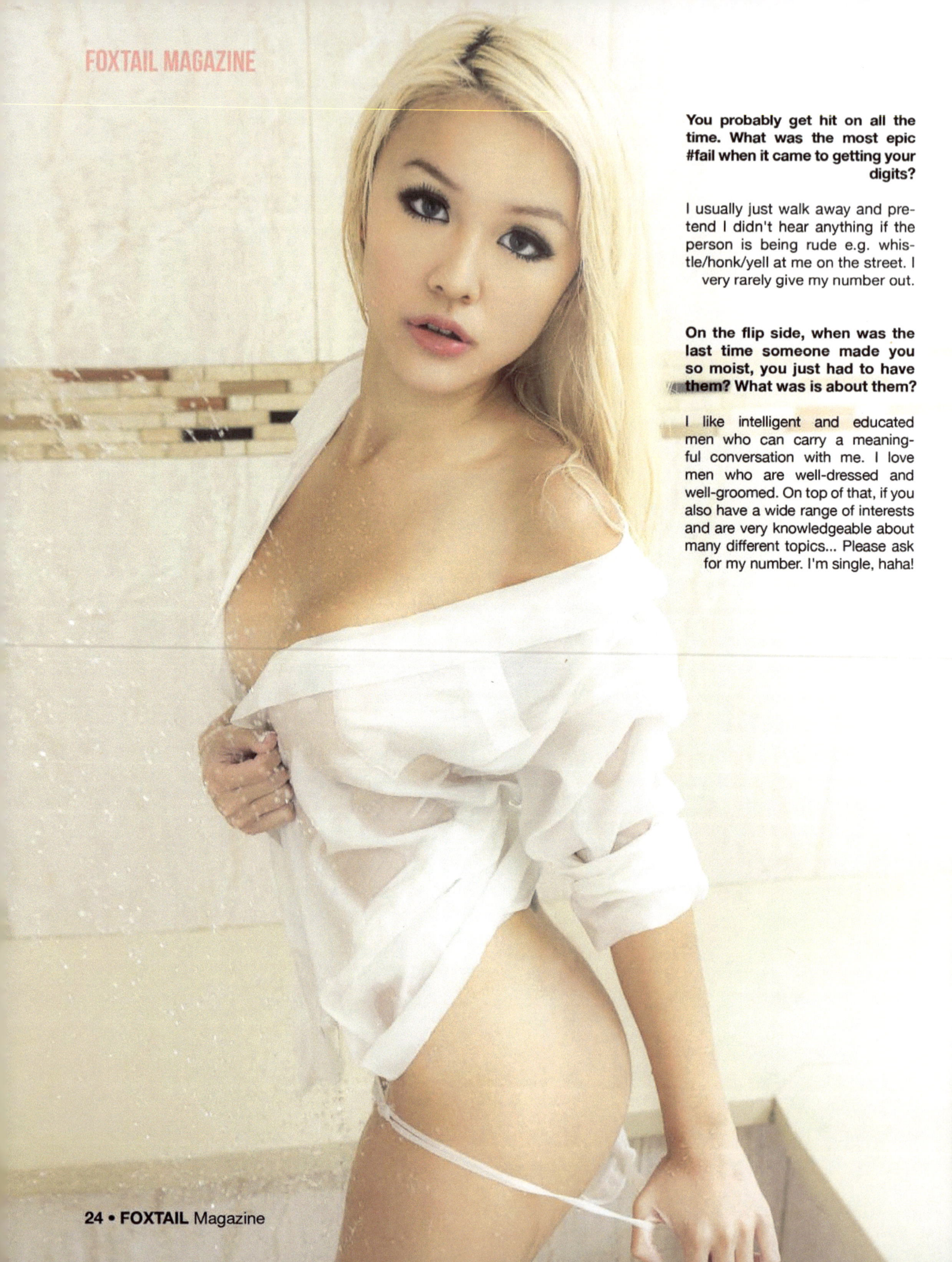

You probably get hit on all the time. What was the most epic #fail when it came to getting your digits?

I usually just walk away and pretend I didn't hear anything if the person is being rude e.g. whistle/honk/yell at me on the street. I very rarely give my number out.

On the flip side, when was the last time someone made you so moist, you just had to have them? What was is about them?

I like intelligent and educated men who can carry a meaningful conversation with me. I love men who are well-dressed and well-groomed. On top of that, if you also have a wide range of interests and are very knowledgeable about many different topics... Please ask for my number. I'm single, haha!

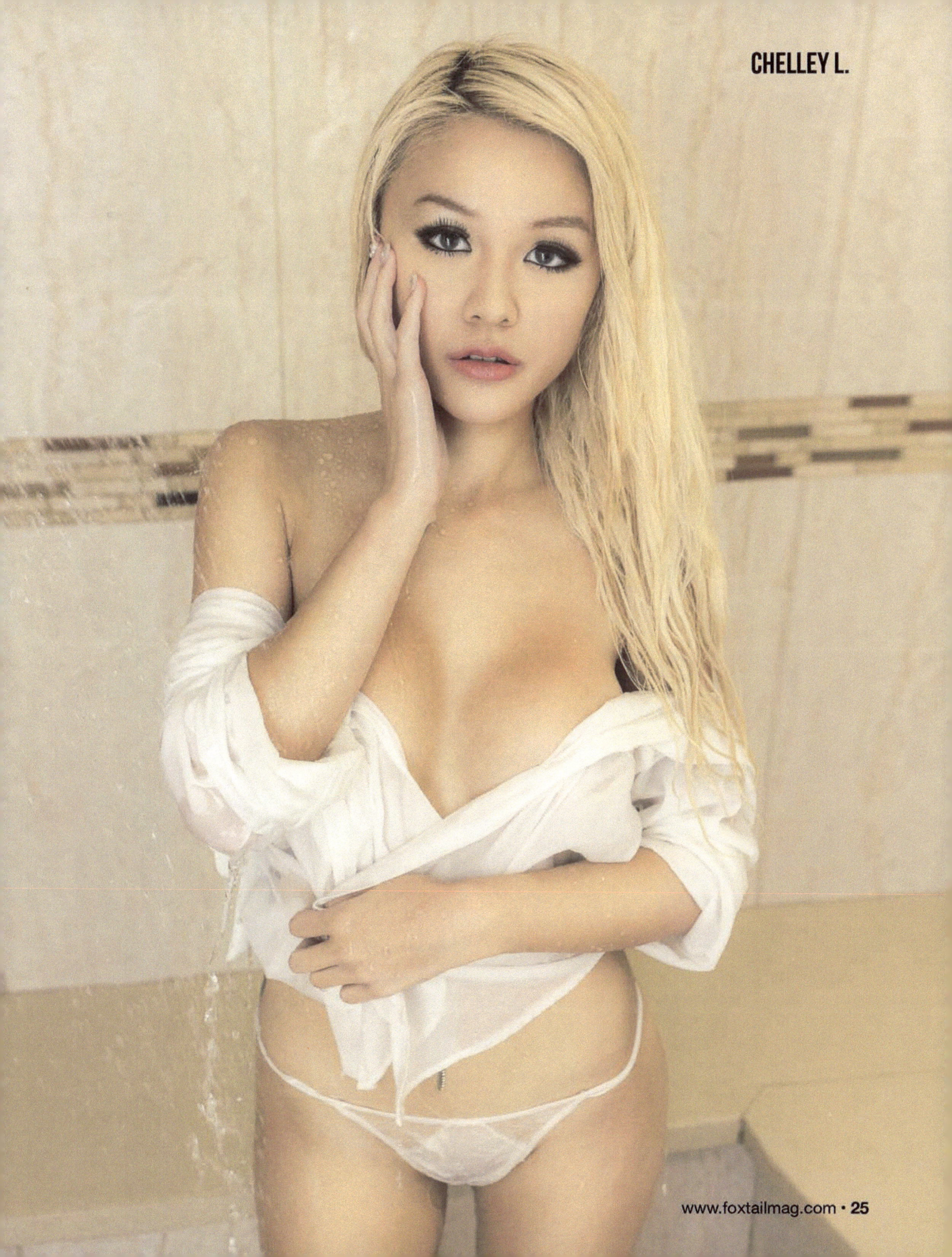

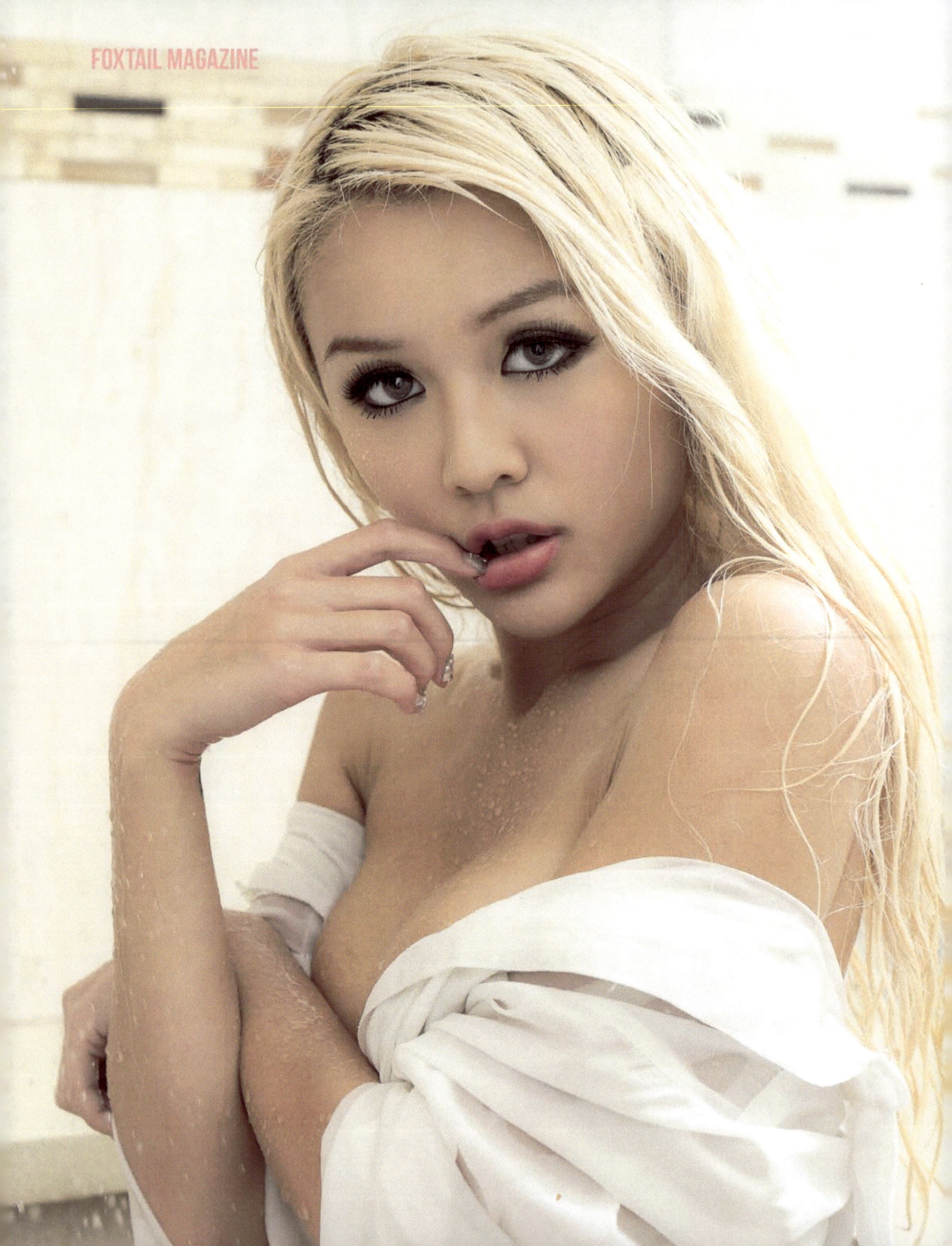

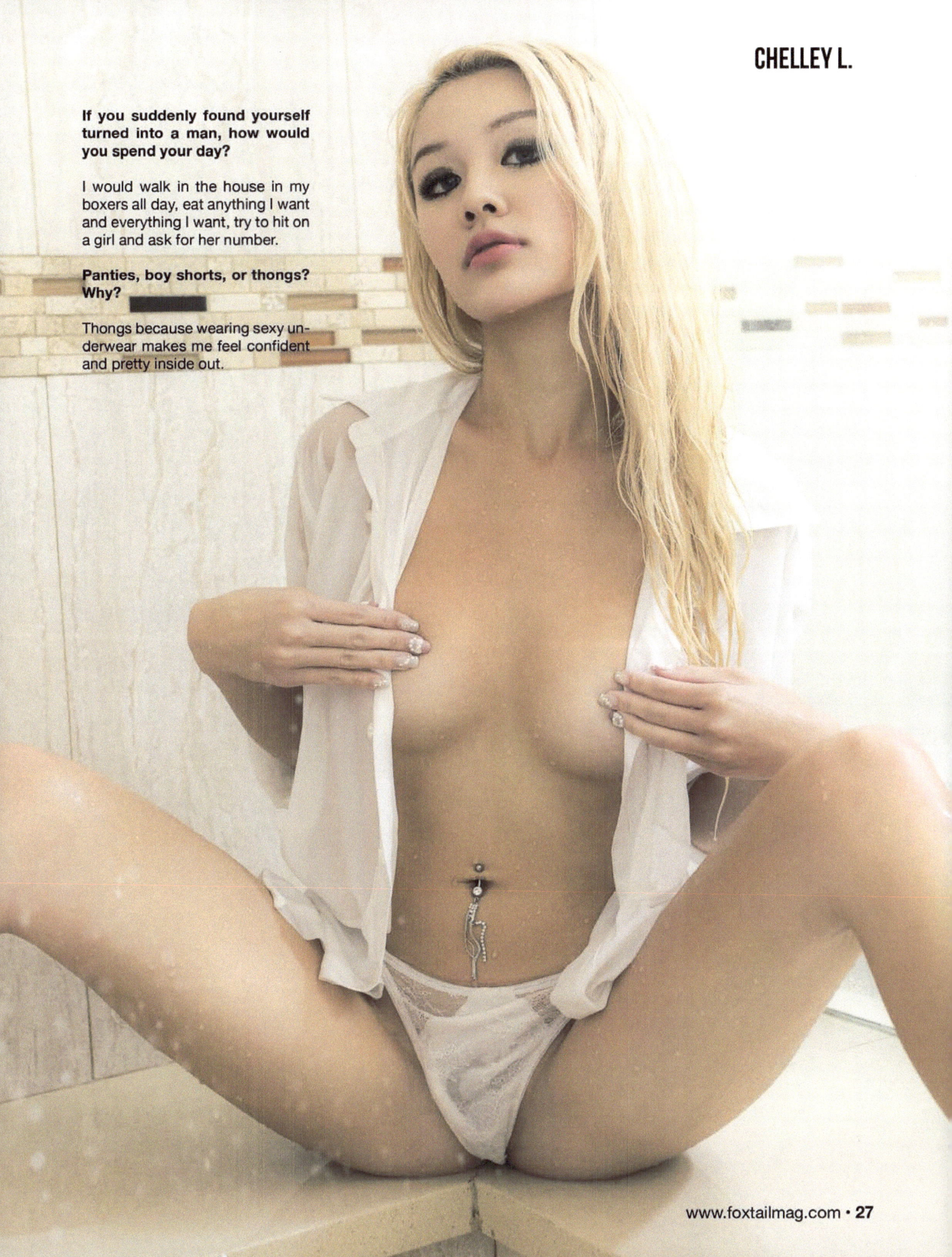

JESSICA KELLY

Photography by Murder City Angles

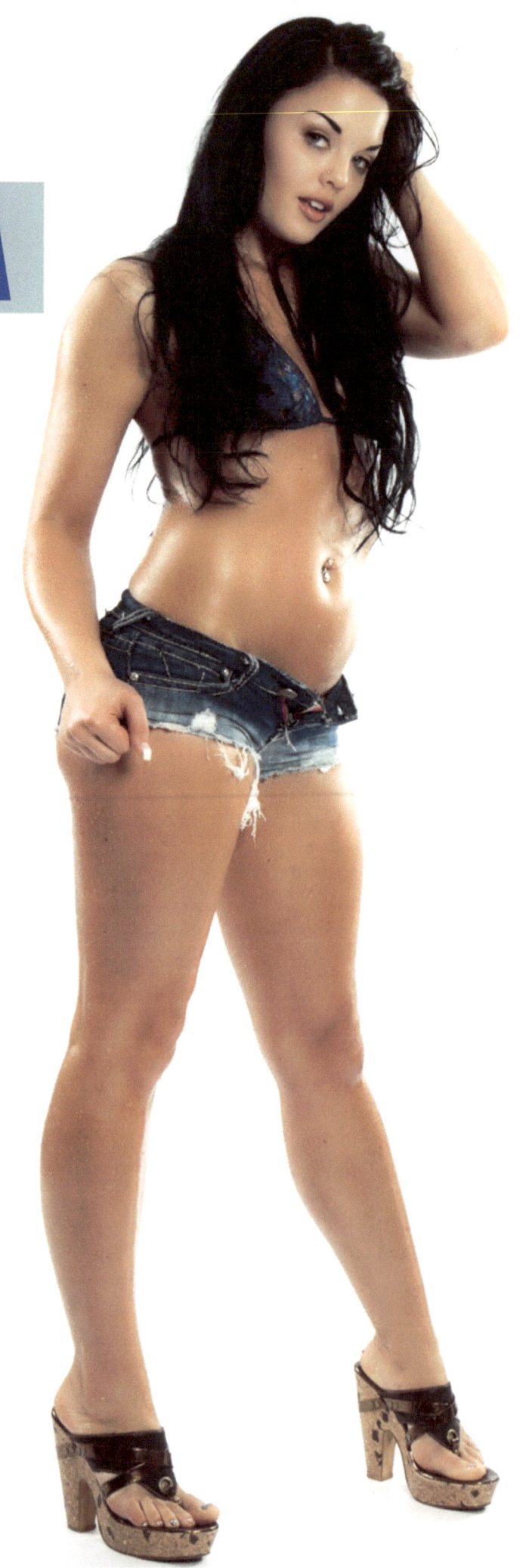

Age: 27

Height: 5'4"

Weight: 130 lbs.

Measurements: 34 - 26 - 36

Nationality: Canadian

Location: Victoria, BC, Canada

Facebook: jessicakellymodel

Instagram: @jessicakellyofficial

Profession: Business Owner

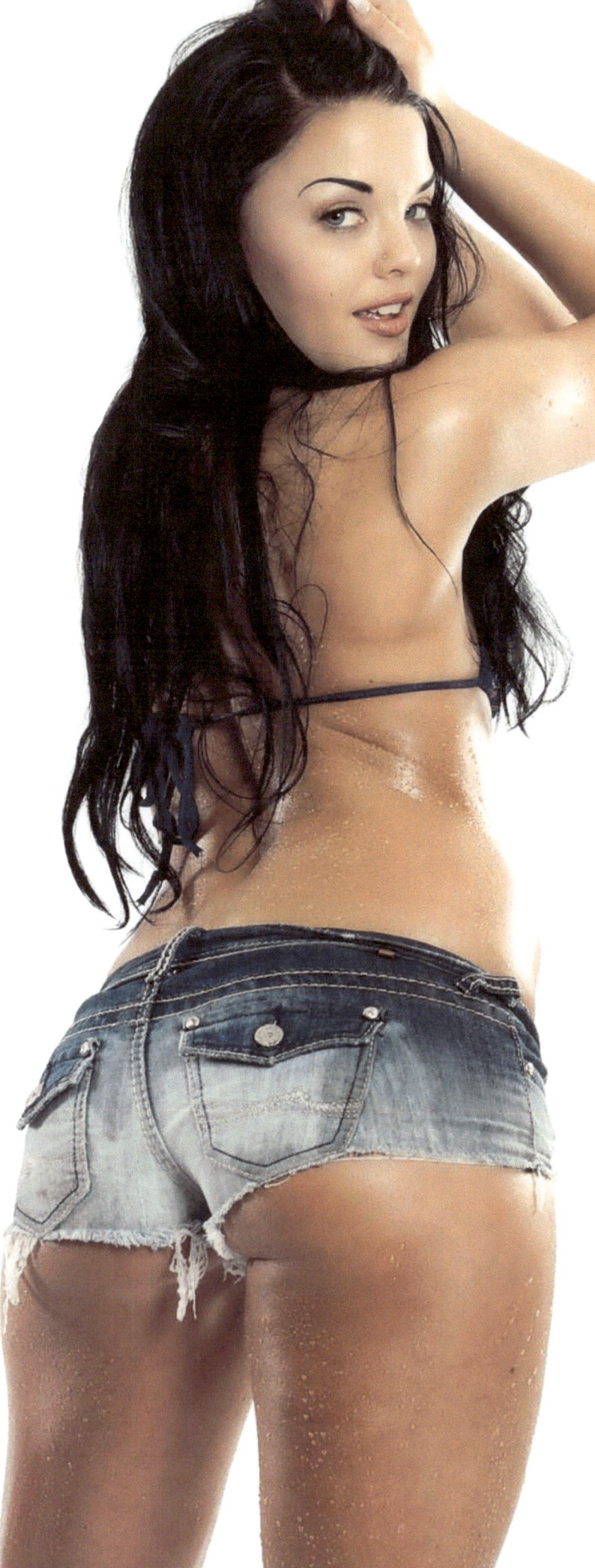

JESSICA KELLY

How do you handle people you don't like?

If I don't like you, I'll just ignore you. I don't get myself wrapped up with petty gossip and cat fights. Not worth my time or ruining my night!

Would you rather be smart and ugly or dumb and beautiful?

Oohhh... My answer would be smart and ugly, but, can I add the clause that I get to make an appointment at Mac for a make-up demonstration?

Do you have a sexual fantasy no one else knows about?

Well, I don't have a whole "fantasy" planned out, but there are a few choice adventures that I may want to partake in. ;)

What's the difference between sex and making love?

Sex is meaningless, last-call, don't-wanna-date-you, just-wanna-do-you sex. Making love is when there is passion and emotion and feelings. I'd choose making love over sex anyday.

If you suddenly found yourself turned into a man, how would you spend your day?

Being a man would be a blast! I would be such a pig. I'd spend my day doing all the fun boy stuff I love – shooting guns, mudding trucks, and I'd have all my hot guy friends with me :)

FOXTAIL MAGAZINE

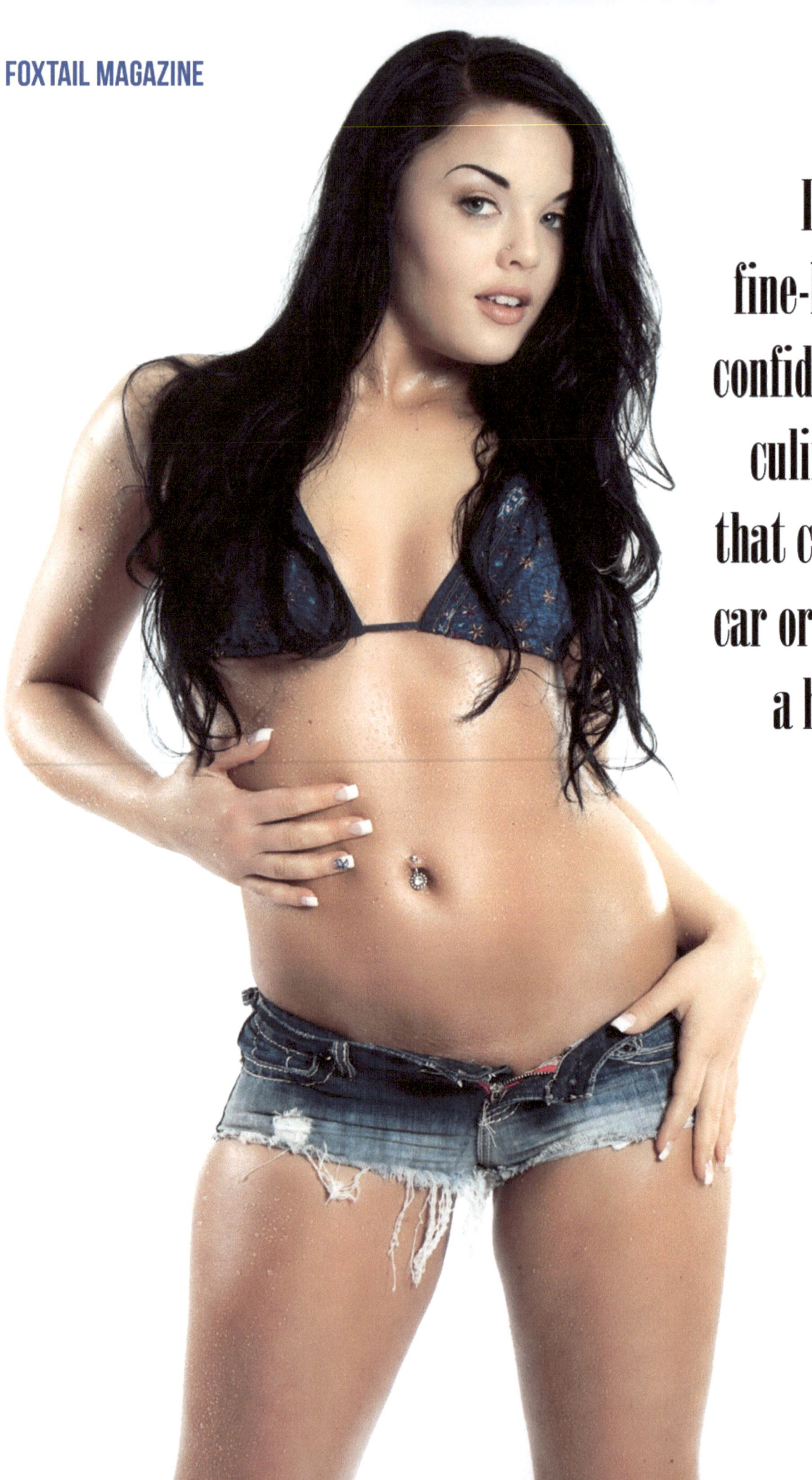

I like fine-looking, confident, masculine men that can fix my car or build me a house.

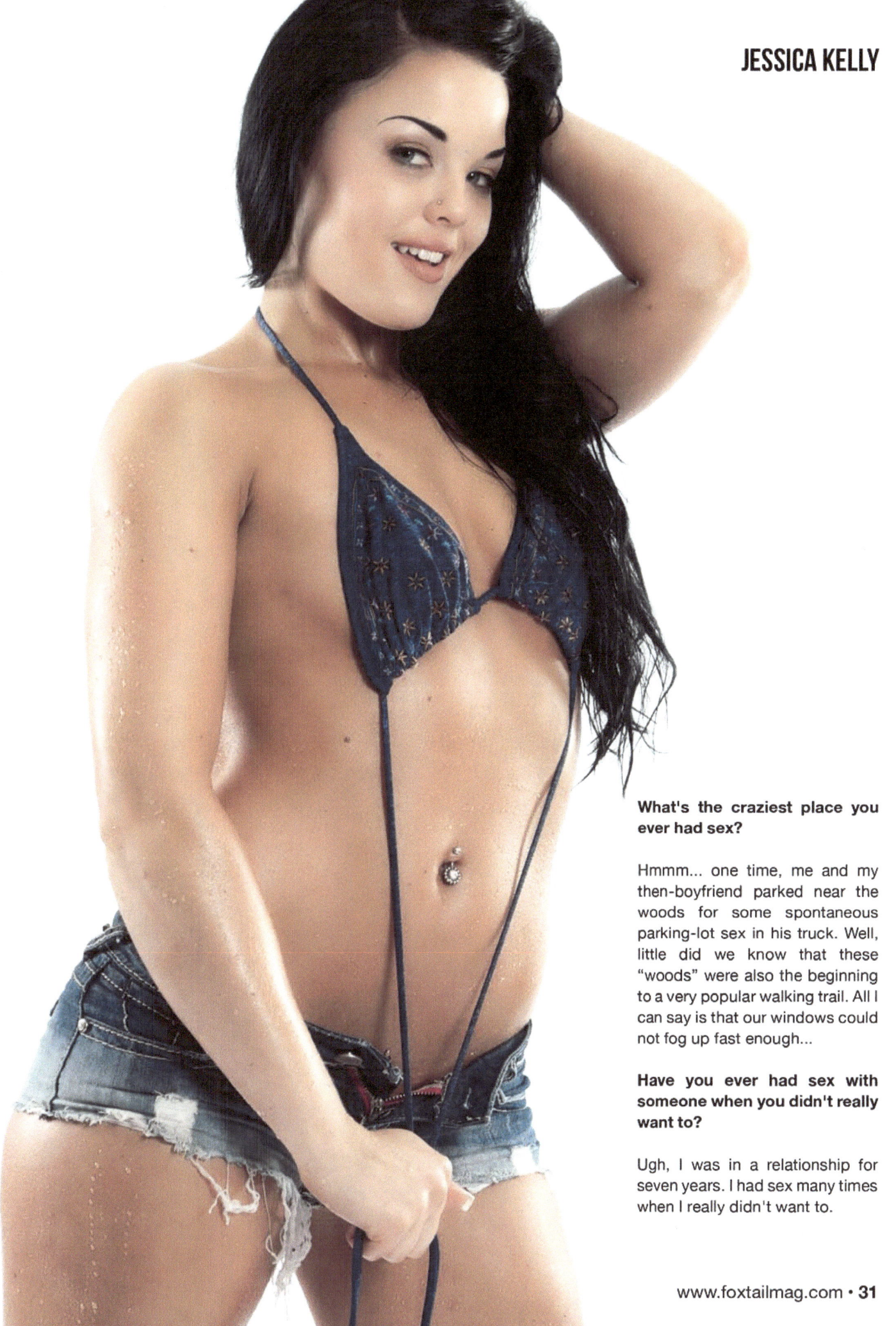

JESSICA KELLY

What's the craziest place you ever had sex?

Hmmm... one time, me and my then-boyfriend parked near the woods for some spontaneous parking-lot sex in his truck. Well, little did we know that these "woods" were also the beginning to a very popular walking trail. All I can say is that our windows could not fog up fast enough...

Have you ever had sex with someone when you didn't really want to?

Ugh, I was in a relationship for seven years. I had sex many times when I really didn't want to.

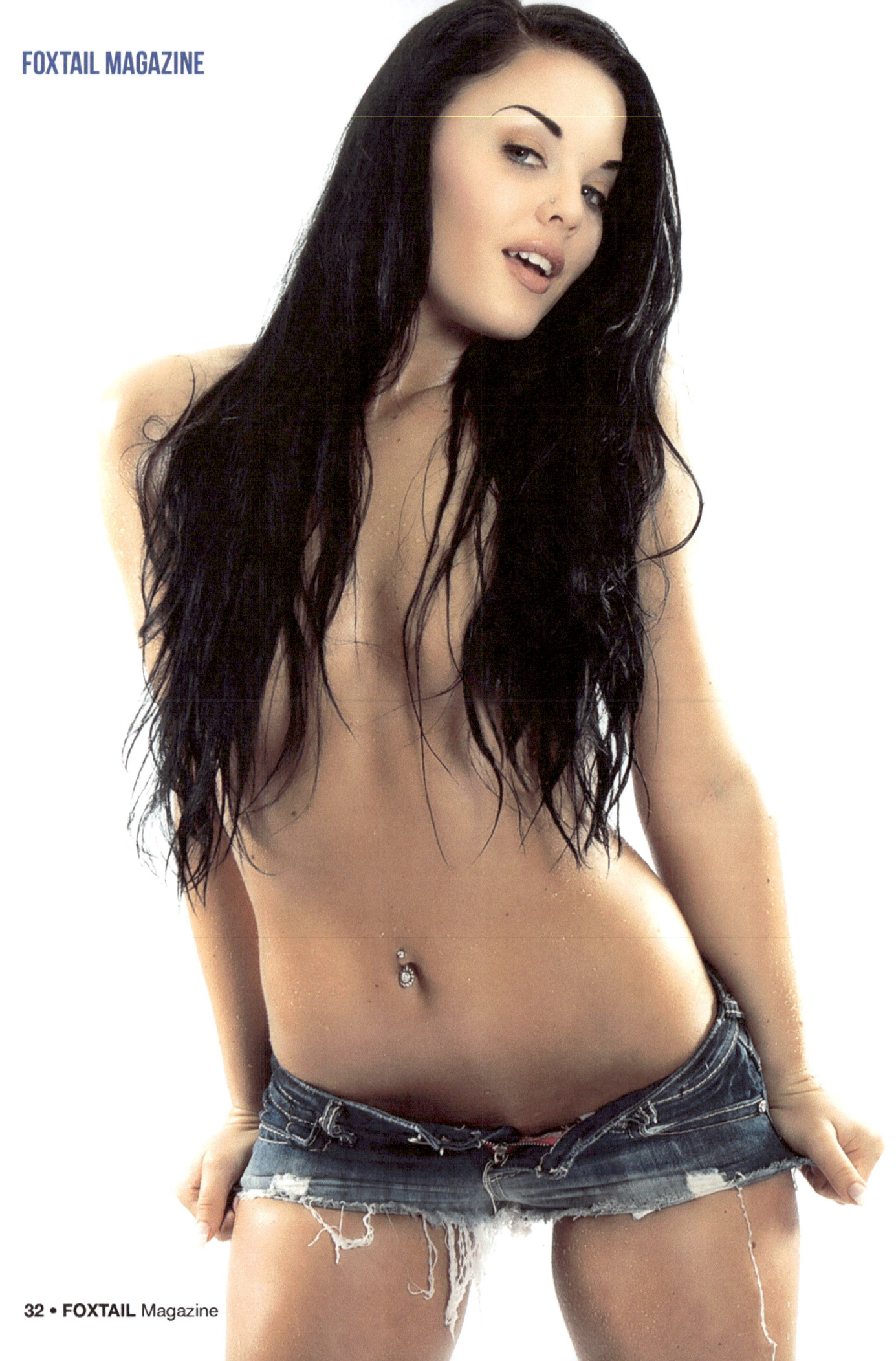

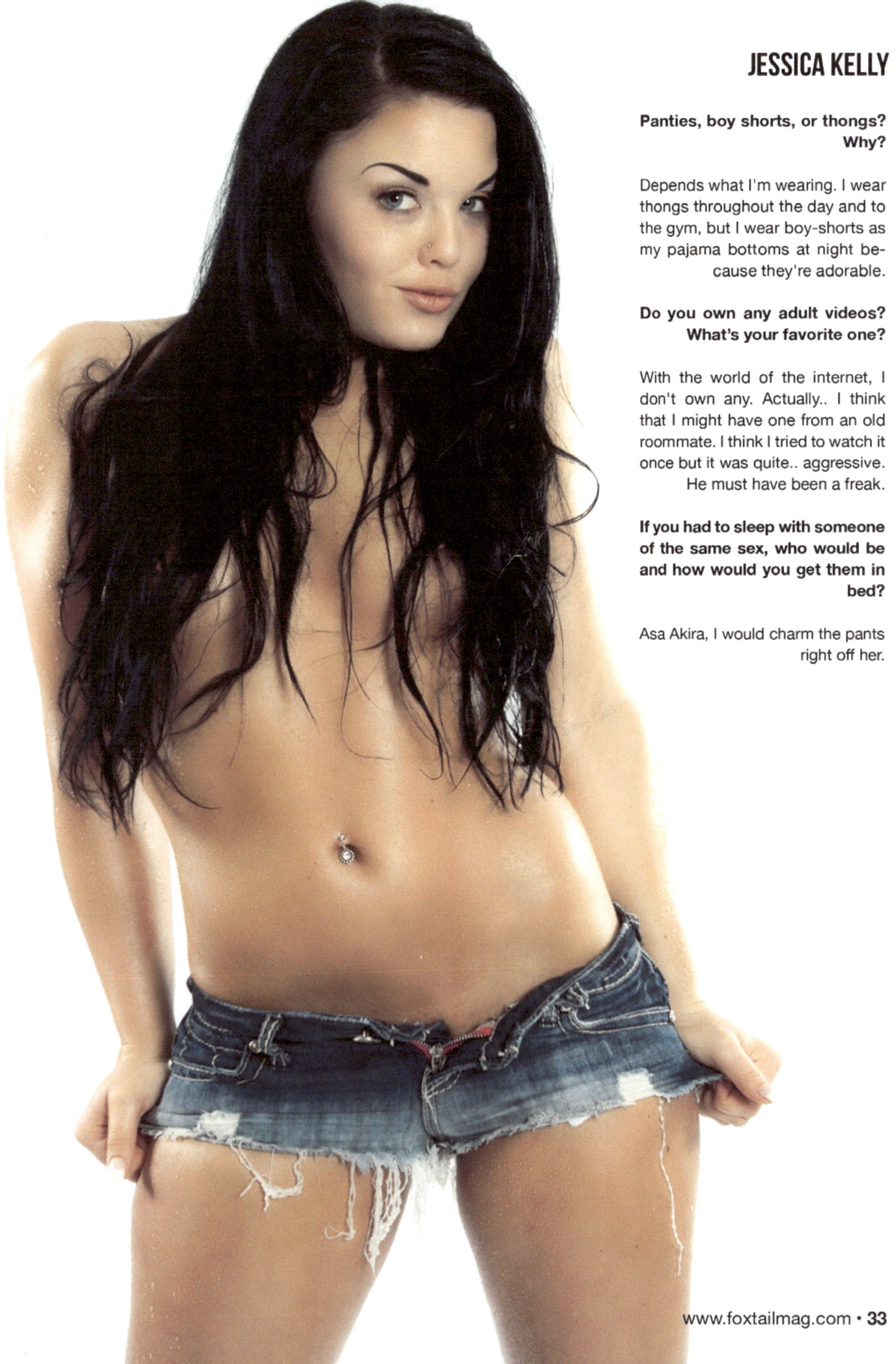

JESSICA KELLY

Panties, boy shorts, or thongs? Why?

Depends what I'm wearing. I wear thongs throughout the day and to the gym, but I wear boy-shorts as my pajama bottoms at night because they're adorable.

Do you own any adult videos? What's your favorite one?

With the world of the internet, I don't own any. Actually.. I think that I might have one from an old roommate. I think I tried to watch it once but it was quite.. aggressive. He must have been a freak.

If you had to sleep with someone of the same sex, who would be and how would you get them in bed?

Asa Akira, I would charm the pants right off her.

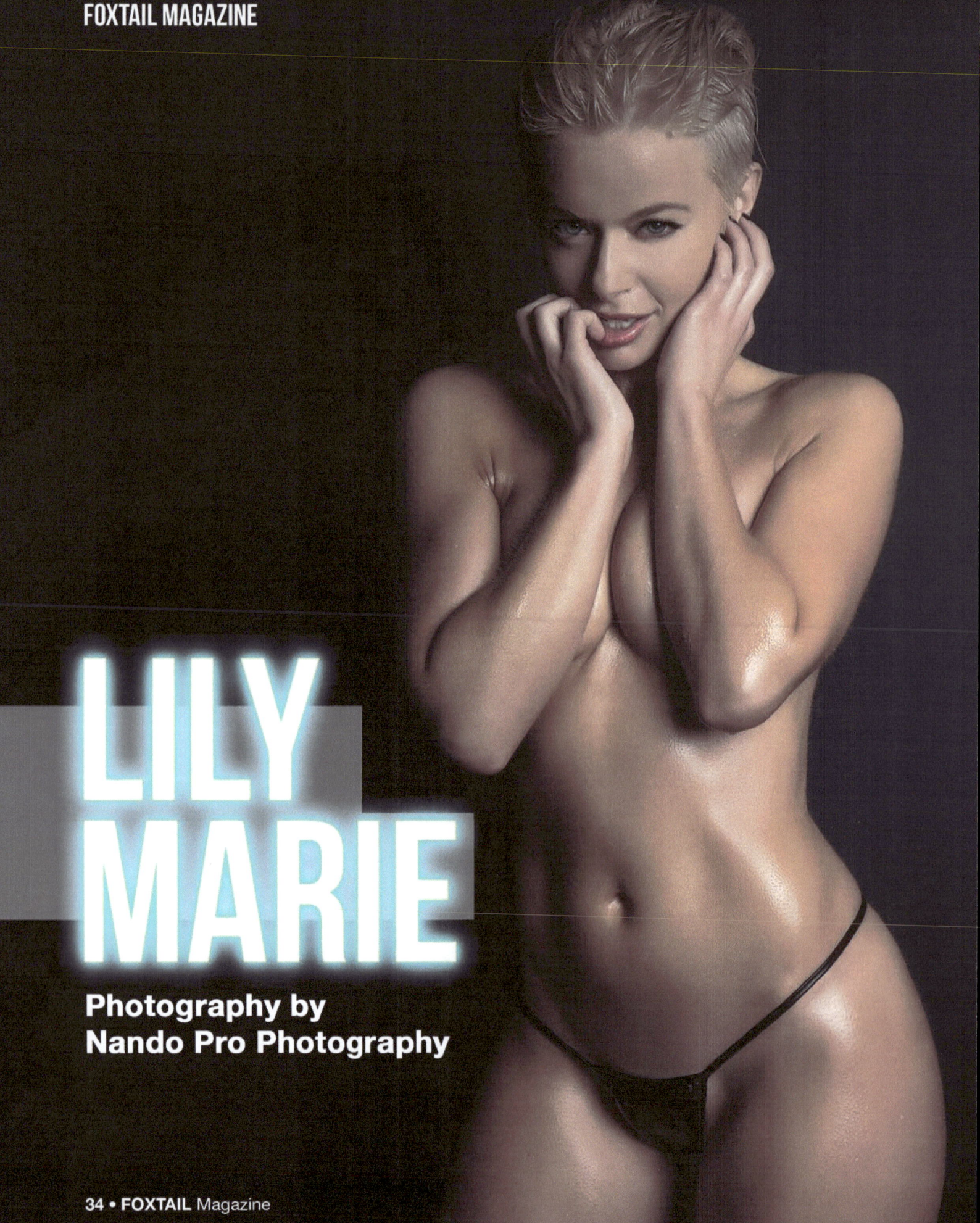

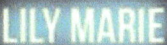

Age: 26

Height: 5'0"

Weight: 105 lbs.

Measurements: 32B - 25 - 35

Ethinicity: Sicilian, Irish

Location: Boston, MA

Relationship Status: Single

Instagram: Lily.MarieXoXo

Profession: Model/Hairstylist

www.foxtailmag.com • 35

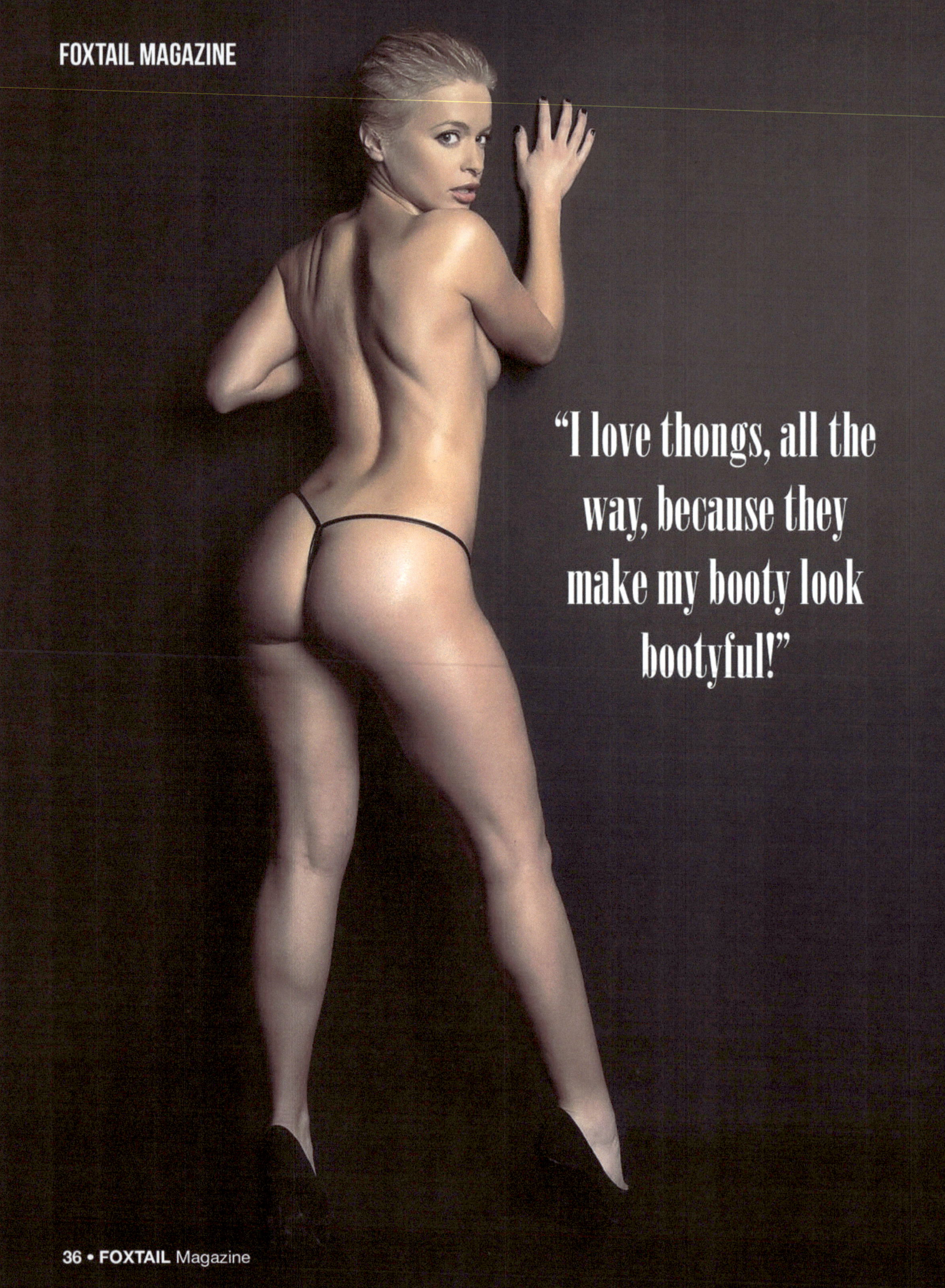

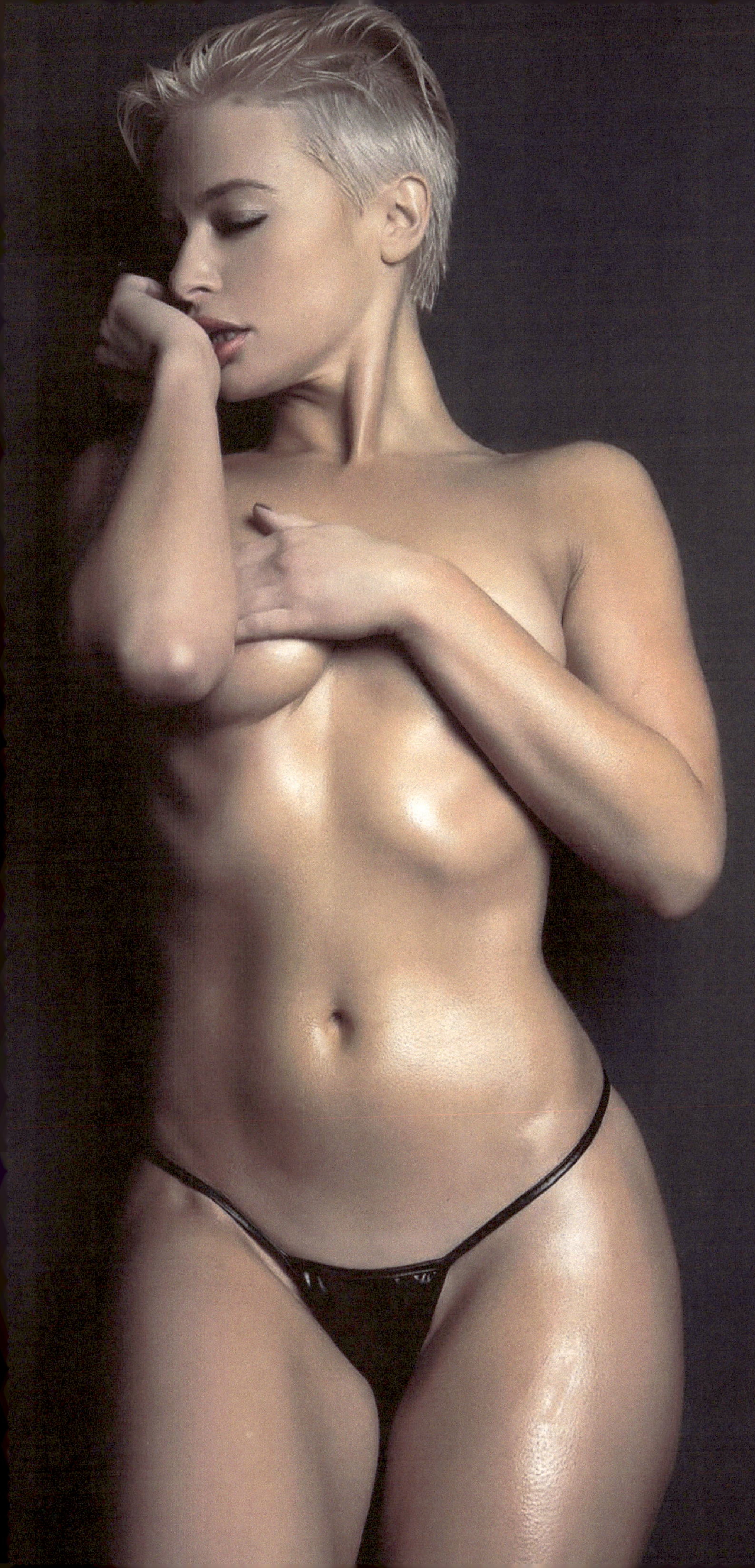

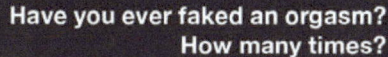

Have you ever faked an orgasm? How many times?

Haha maybe... Come on! A girl would be lying if she said she never faked one before. But, let's not get technical, haha!

Would you consider yourself popular, semi-famous, or famous?

I'm a dork. A pretty dork. I will go with popular, haha!

Kill, Marry, Fuck? (Please list one celebrity for each category)

Haha, oh man! Let's see. Well there is no question I would have sexual relations with Mark Wahlberg and marry him too if i had my way! I would have to kill Carrot top! He creeps me out!! He's like the freaking Clown from Stephen King's IT!

If I had _____, I wouldn't have to _____! (Fill in the blanks)

If I had a unicorn, I wouldn't have to dress my dog like one!

You probably get hit on all the time. What was the most epic #fail when it came to getting your digits?

Lol, there are so many classics! I think my favorite one was when this gentlemen proclaimed he had something important to tell me. As he pushed his way through some people to get to me, he proceeded to tell me and I quote " I just had to tell you how amazing your nose is, it's stunning!" Do you have a BF? Can I get your number!?" I anticipated something completely different and when he blurted that out I couldn't help but lose it. I managed to say thank you but quickly turned around and bolted the other way in hysterics. Seriously epic! Lol!

LILY MARIE

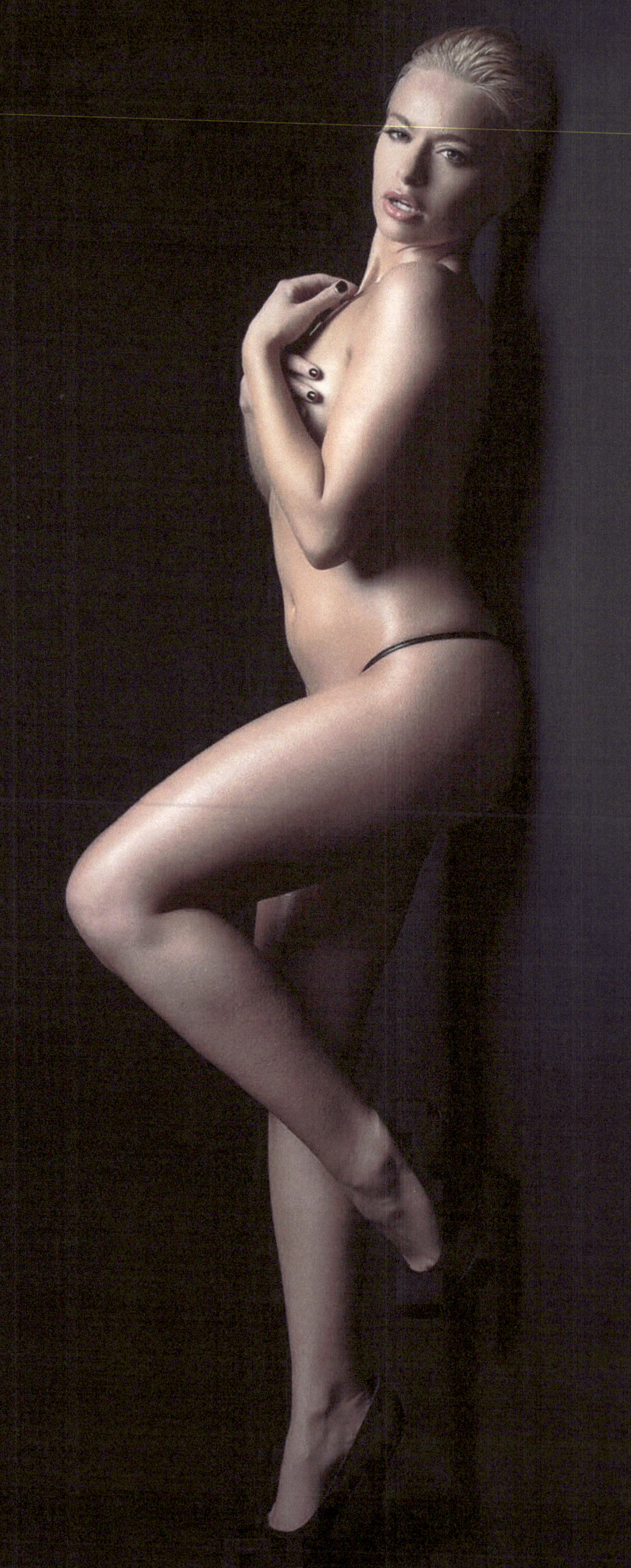

On the flip side, when was the last time someone made you so moist, you just had to have them? What was is about them?

Well... I can tell you the last thing that made me wet and sticky while trying to eat it. I was a slice of watermelon! That's about as dirty as it's gonna get with that question! Haha!

If you suddenly found yourself turned into a man, how would you spend your day?

Oh my god that would be the worst day of my life!! I would definitely spend the day in solitary confinement, hiding in my closet! Lol!

What's the craziest place you ever had sex?

Hmm... Well, obviously I must be pretty boring then, haha!

What turns you on? Turns you off?

A good sense of humor is always a turn on to me. A big turnoff is when a guy is egocentric.

If you had to sleep with someone of the same sex, who would be and how would you get them in bed?

Who? I don't know. That's just scary! Haha, but candy could work!? Like anything chocolate! Bitches love chocolate!

Tell us the wildest sexual fantasy that you've evqer heard. Don't hold out!

I don't understand the whole foot fetish thing, it creeps me out! Feet are gross! I mean massaging them is one thing but I don't want them in, on, or around me! If you ever try to come to me, asking me to do things with yours or mine, I would literally heave on you and run away! Lol!

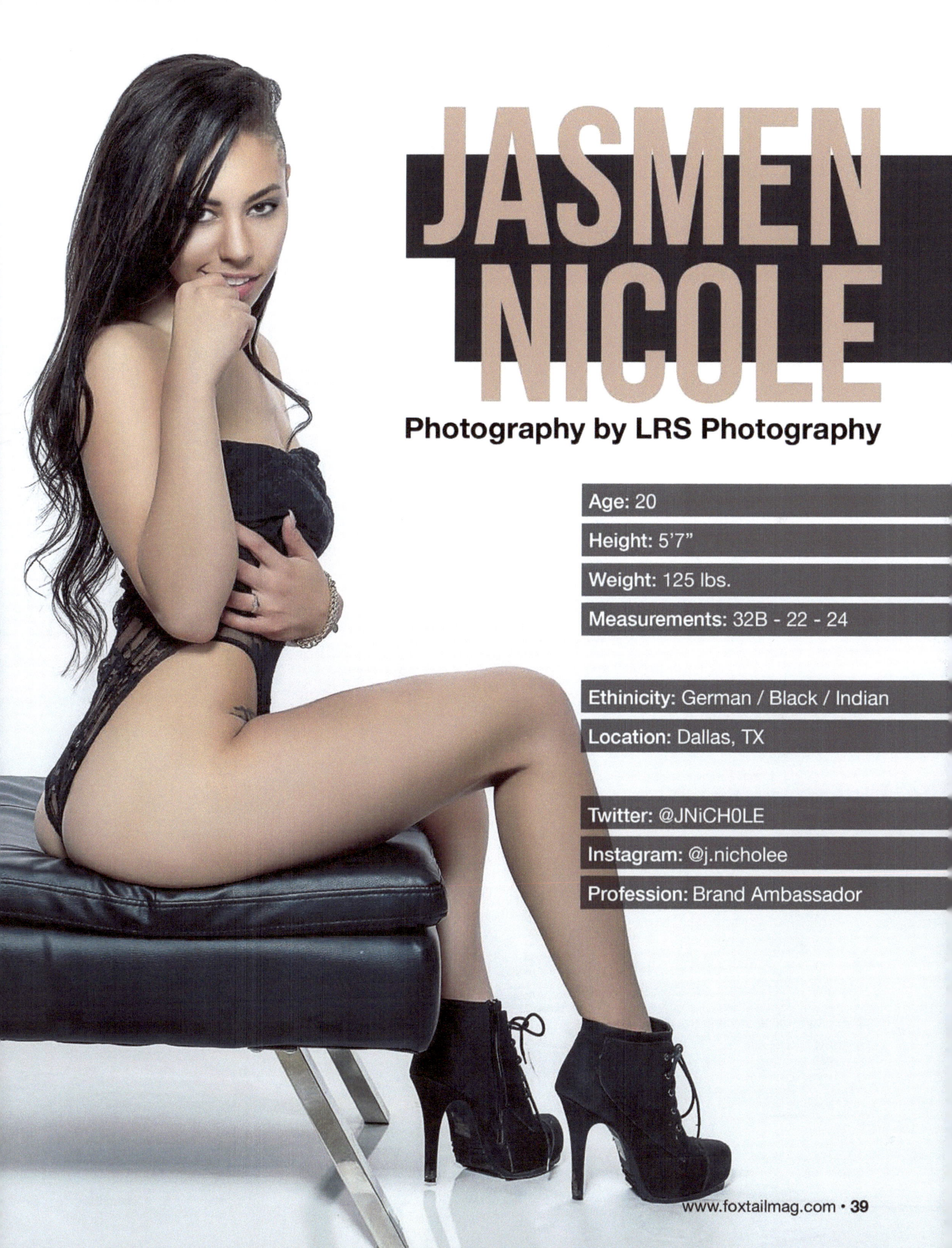

JASMEN NICOLE

Photography by LRS Photography

- Age: 20
- Height: 5'7"
- Weight: 125 lbs.
- Measurements: 32B - 22 - 24

- Ethinicity: German / Black / Indian
- Location: Dallas, TX

- Twitter: @JNiCH0LE
- Instagram: @j.nicholee
- Profession: Brand Ambassador

FOXTAIL MAGAZINE

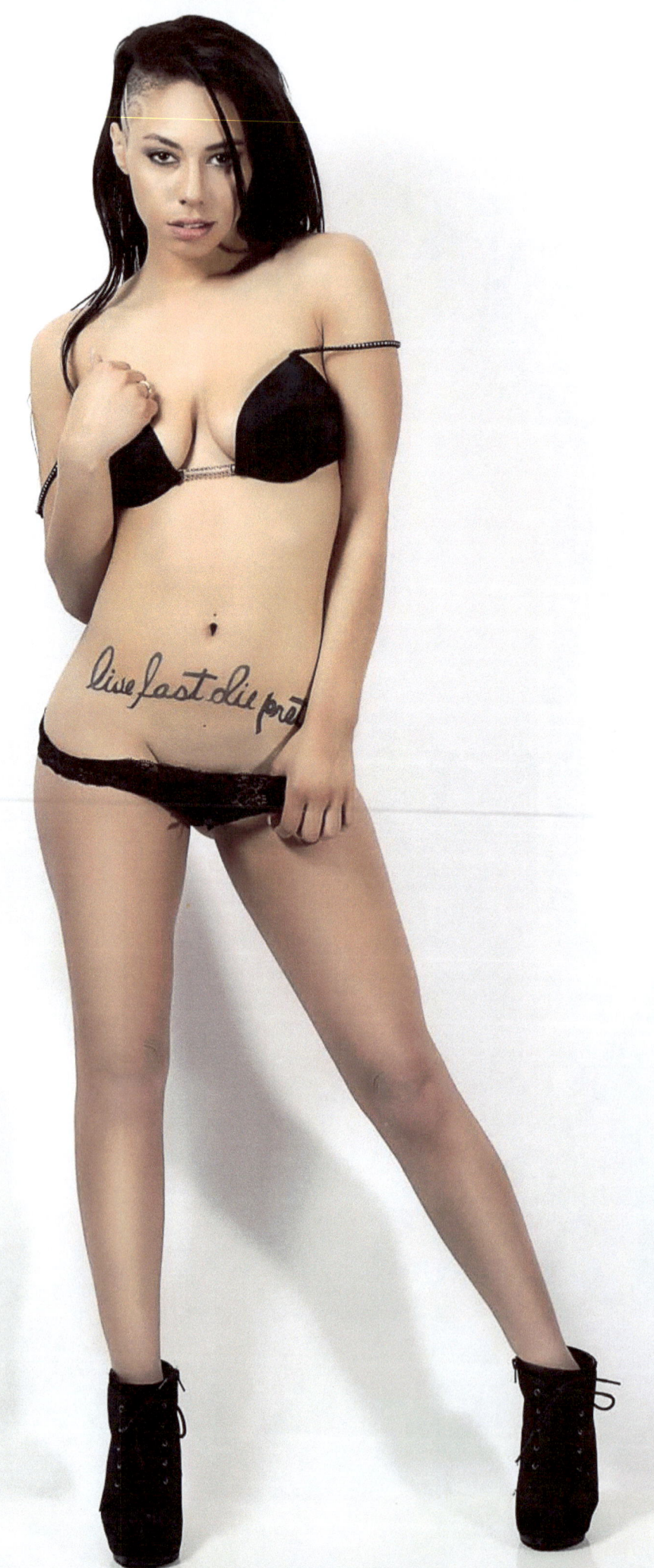

Have you ever faked an orgasm? How many times?

Haha, who hasnt? It's mostly when I'm just not feeling the dude and I want it to be over. I'd say about 4 times.

Would you consider yourself popular, semi-famous, or famous?

Maybe popular, but that's not why I'm in this industry, I got big plans for it (;

Kill, Marry, Fuck? (Please list one celebrity for each category)

Kill young thuggery because he's so damn annoying. Marry Big Sean because I feel like his last album was about my life. Fuck Trey songz, because I mean it's Trey fucking Songz, lol.

If I had _____, I wouldn't have to _____! (Fill in the blanks)

If I had _a jet_, I wouldn't have to _____drive___! (Fill in the blanks)

You probably get hit on all the time. What was the most epic #fail when it came to getting your digits?

The whole "I swear I'm not trying to hit on You but.." like obviously you are trying to hit on me.. lying already and we just met, NEXT.

On the flip side, when was the last time someone made you so moist, you just had to have them? What was is about them?

He was just light skin with a sexy body and that my weakness.. It was game over, lol!

If you suddenly found yourself turned into a man, how would you spend your day?

Hitting on all the beautiful women with a nice ass (;

40 • FOXTAIL Magazine

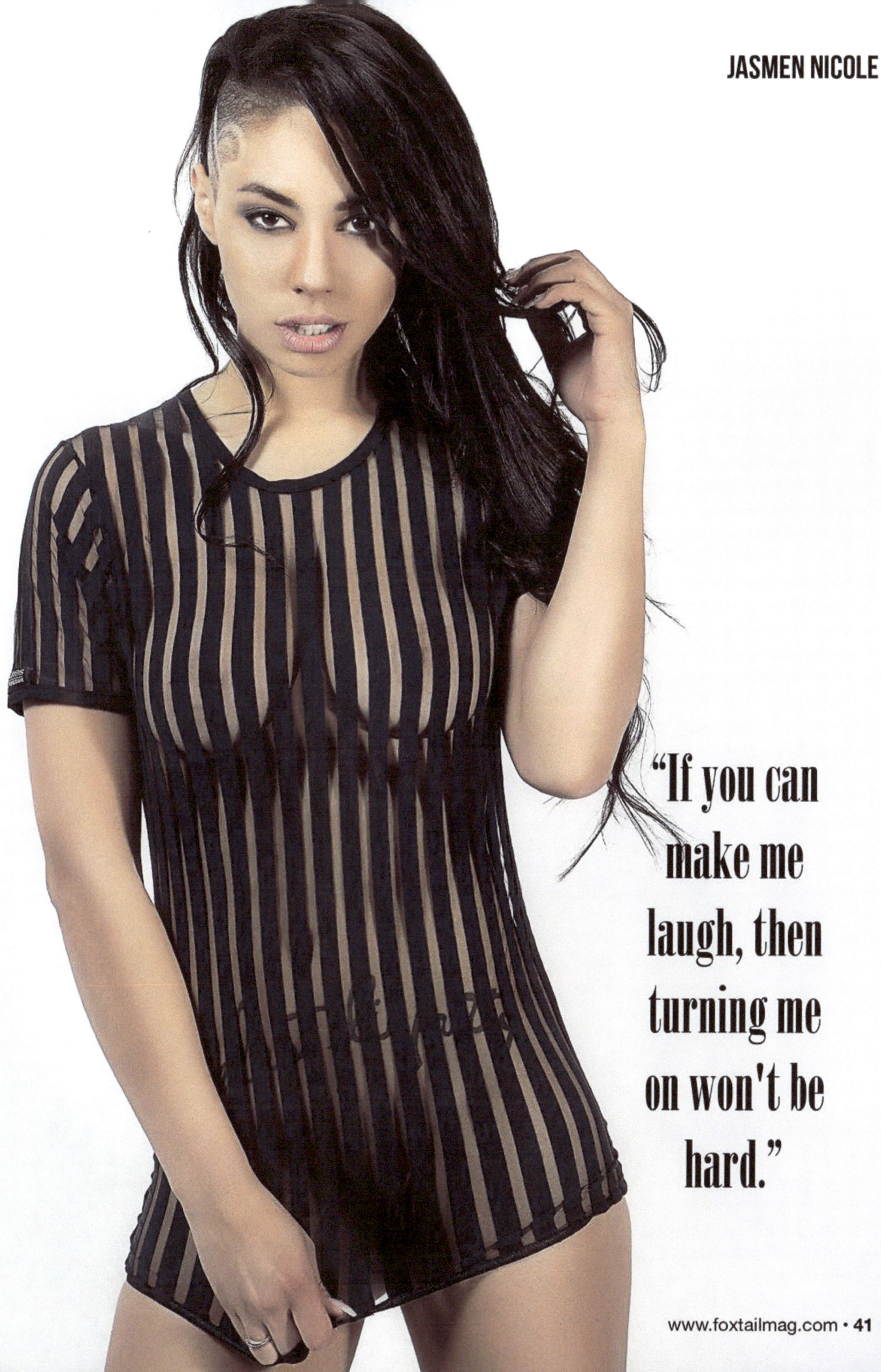

JASMEN NICOLE

"If you can make me laugh, then turning me on won't be hard."

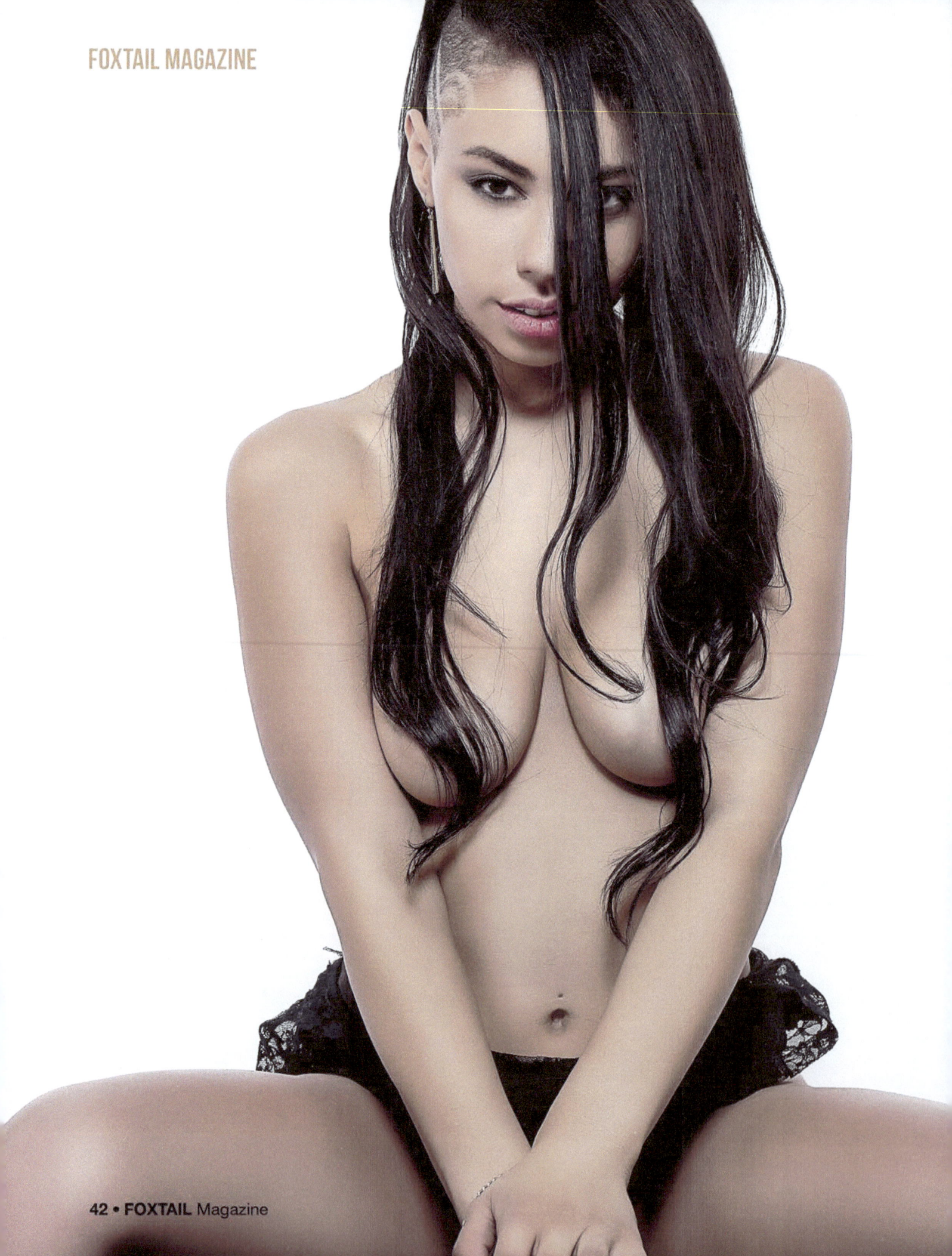

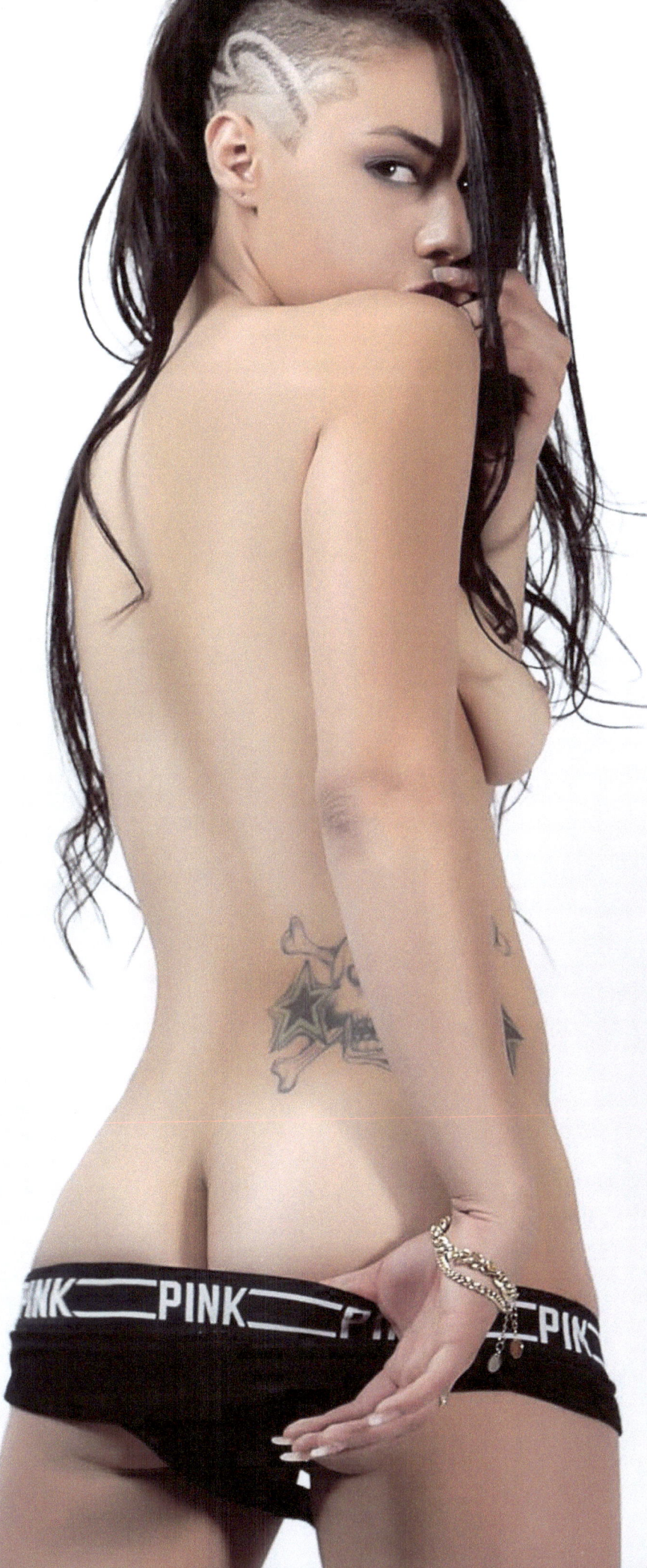

JASMEN NICOLE

What's the craziest place you ever had sex?

On a boat, in the middle of the lake. it was hot, definetly do it again.

What turns you on? Turns you off?

My turn on is guy that is funny without trying and can hold a conversation. If you can make me laugh turning me on won't be hard. Turn of is a guy that is too pushy or who you can tell is try WAY too hard. That's not cute boys.

Panties, boy shorts, or thongs? Why?

Boy shorts because they're so comfortable and always make my ass look good. (I'm an ass type of girl, if you can't tell.

If you had to sleep with someone of the same sex, who would be and how would you get them in bed?

It would be John legends wife, Christy Tiegen. I would get her drunk and just dance with her all night and then nonchalantly just feel her ass and nice tits. She'd probably feel some type of way and you know the rest (;

Tell us the wildest sexual fantasy that you've ever heard. Don't hold out!

Okay I heard a dude say that he wanted to watch his dad fuck a girl, and then he fuck her right after. I don't think that's right yall.. do yall agree? haha!

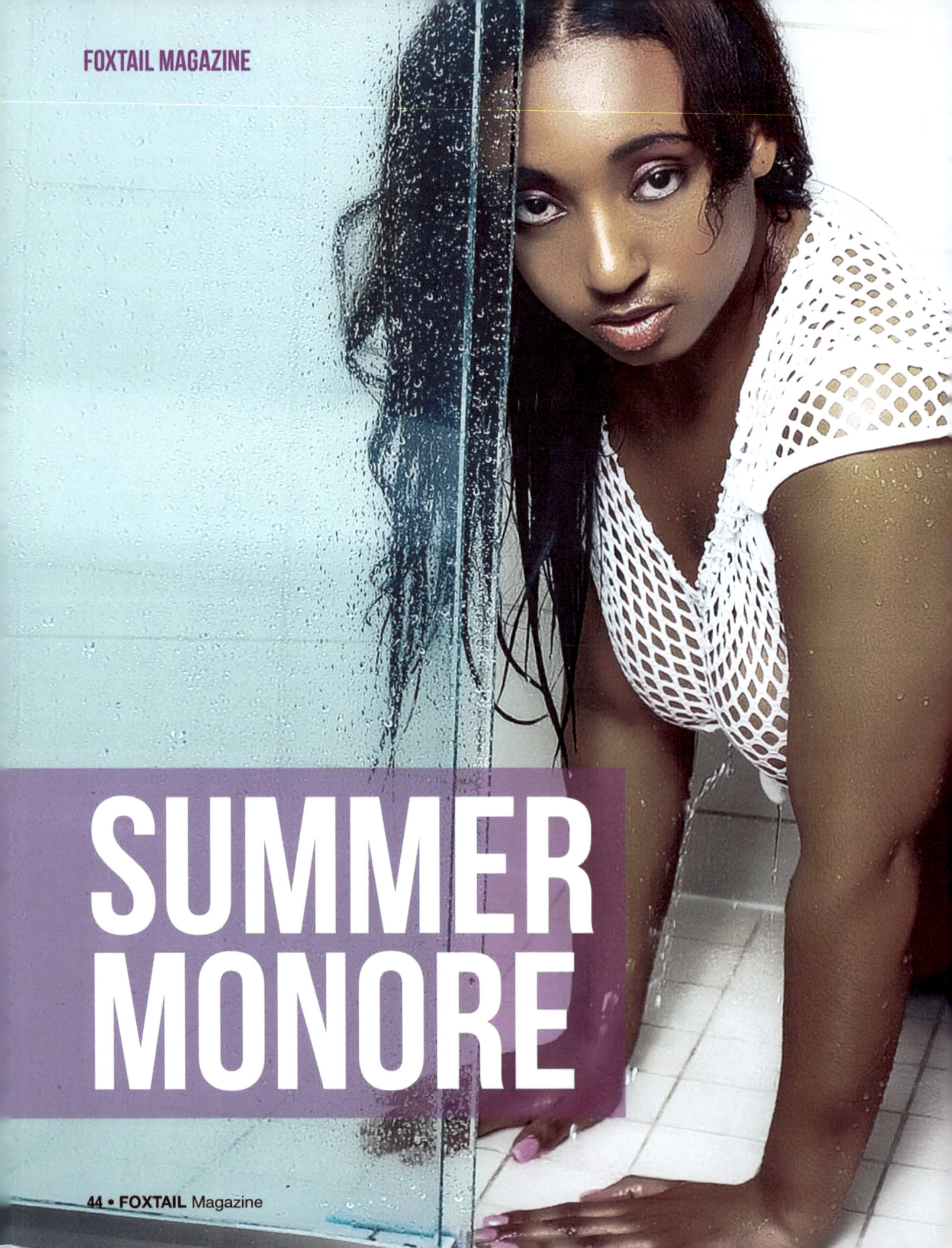

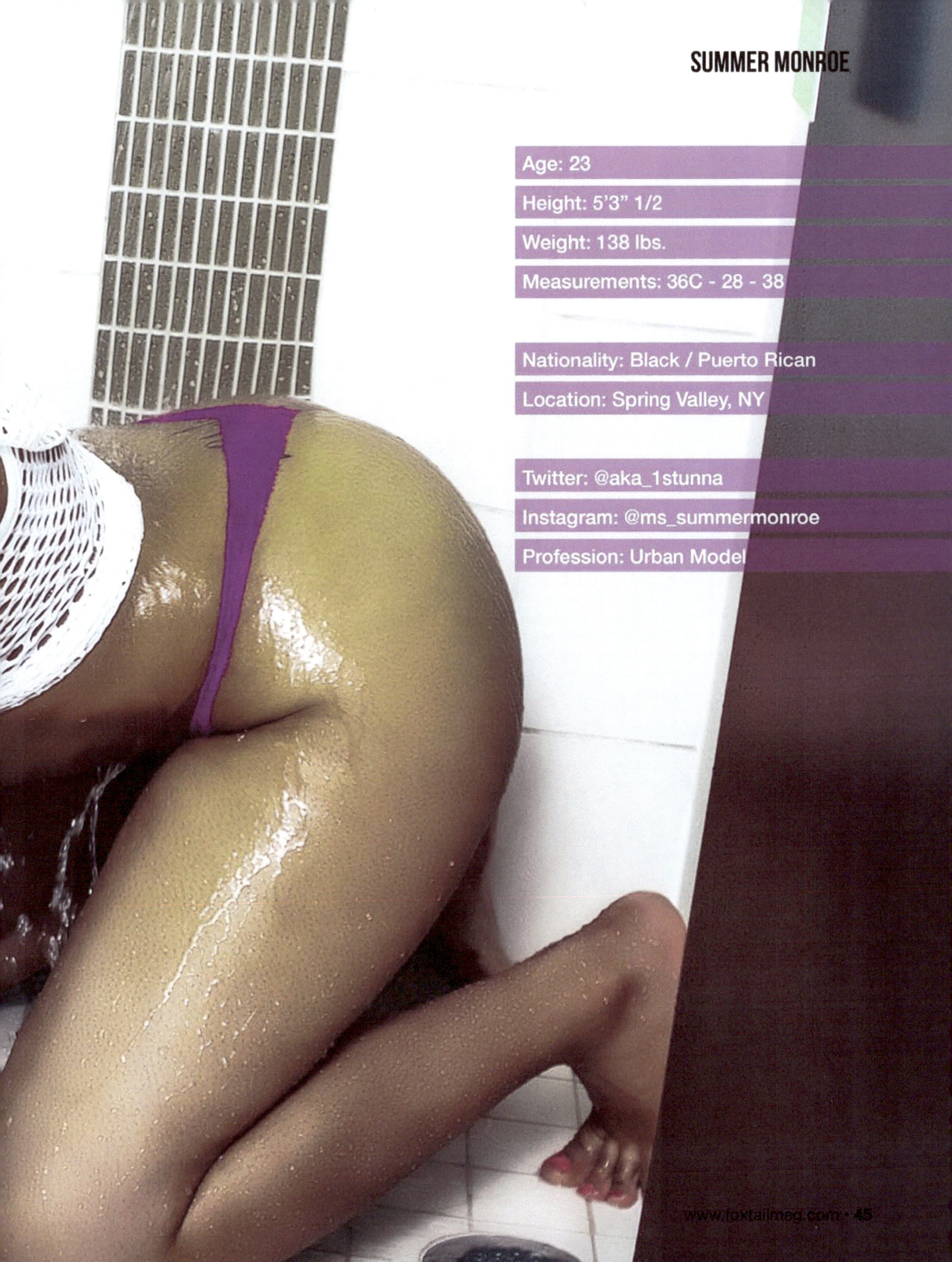

FOXTAIL MAGAZINE

How do you handle people you don't like?

I look right past them but still wish well.

How do you set the mood when you're looking for some action?

I either act silly, freaky or act up (like catching a attitude).

Do you have a sexual fantasy no one else knows about?

Yes, watching another couples have rough sex.

Money, sex, or love? Why?

I say, sex... because it sets the mood no matter what's going on. Good or bad.

If you suddenly found yourself turned into a man, how would you spend your day?

Horny, like a fast rabbit but most of all respectful. And I'd probably wanna some ladies pregnant, lol.

What's the craziest place you ever had sex?

I would say the park, but it wasn't closed off. If some one or somebody would come out either left or right, then they would see us fully

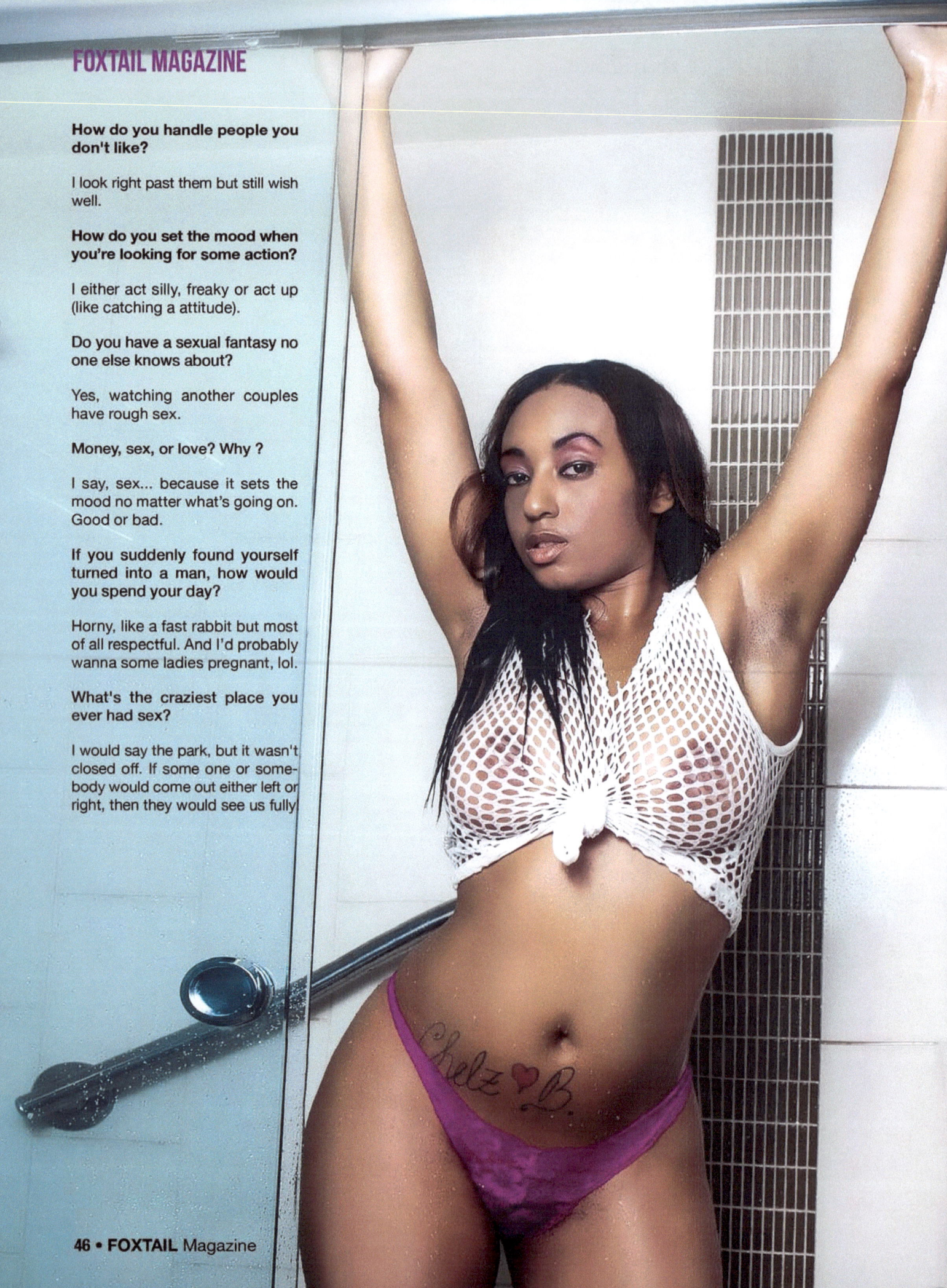

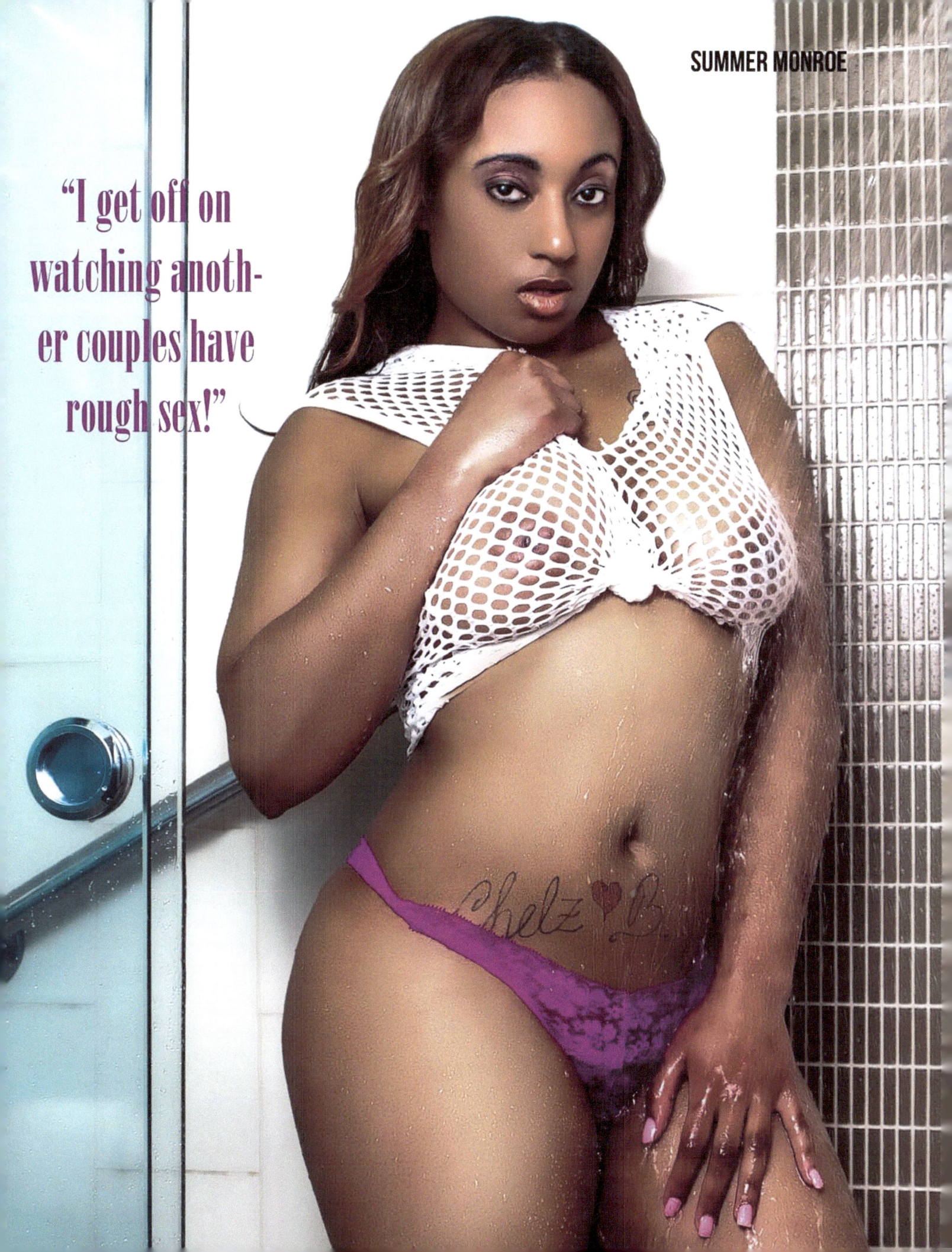

FOXTAIL MAGAZINE

Have you ever had sex with someone when you didn't really want to?

Yes.. but it's crazy because you try to not like it but end up likening it, lol.

What turns you on?

When some can make me laugh and it's genuine, food, porn, sucking on my feet, licking my ear, and females.

Turns you off?

No passion, boring and non communicator, ugly feet and teeth on a female, always talking about them self.

Panties, boy shorts, or thongs? Why?

Thongs but i do wear all, but i love thongs because they make the ass look full and phat.

Do you own any adult videos? What's your favorite one?

No, but i need to get some so I can watch on my flat screen. Now, I just watch them on my phone. I love anything with Wesley Pipes and Jazmine Cashmere.

If you had to sleep with someone of the same sex, who would be and how would you get them in bed?

My two bestfriends, because 2 out of 1 is active and the other hasn't been around like us, imma put it like that lol, But i do know we all would be freaks with each other.

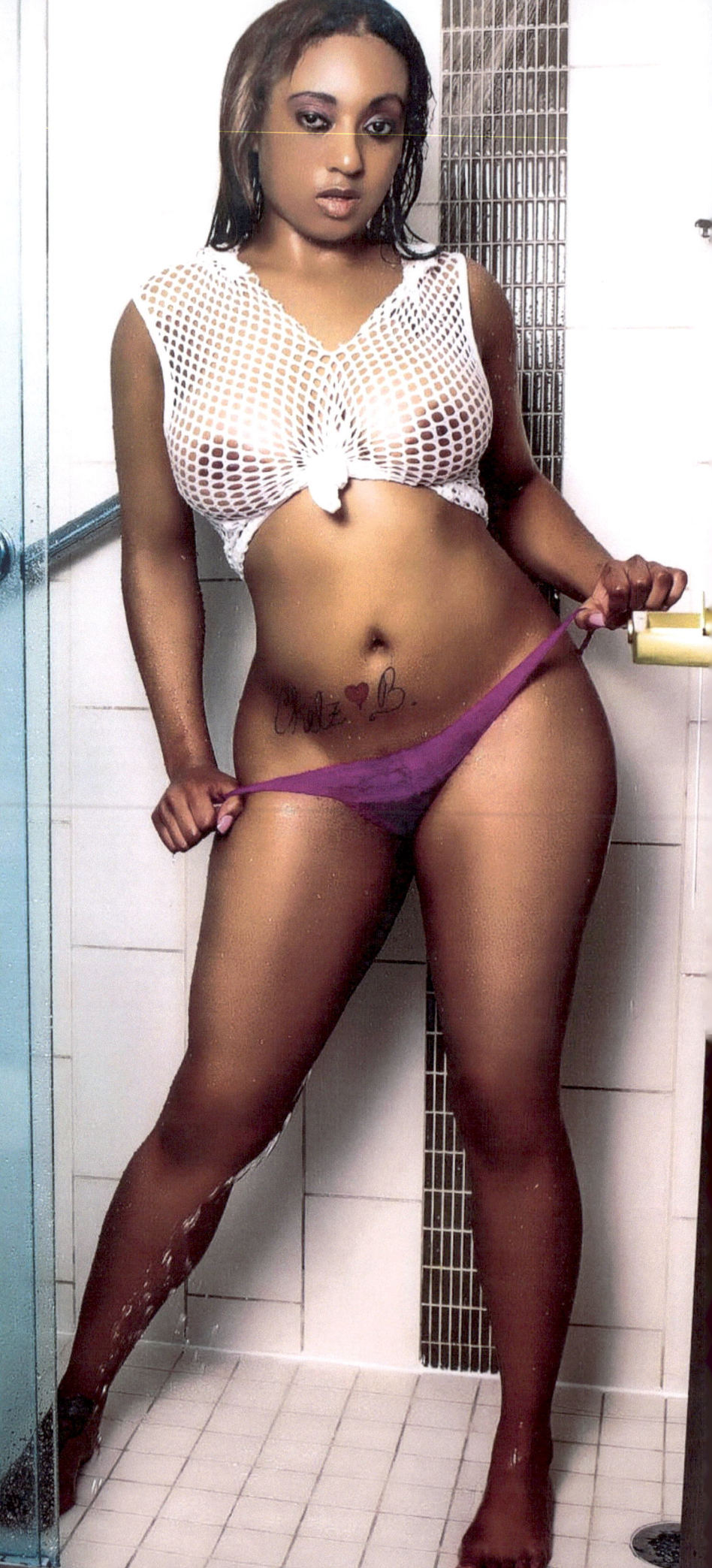

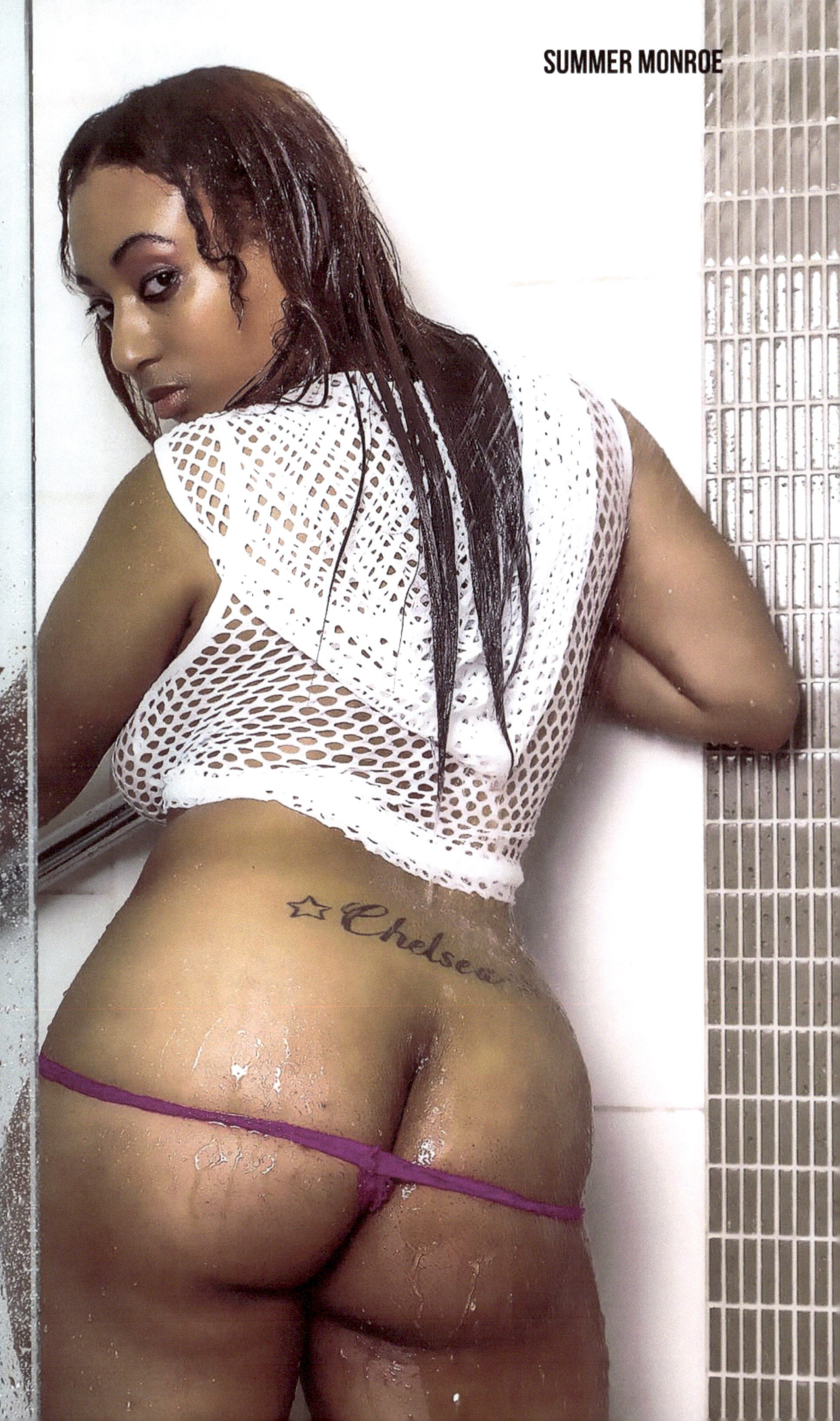

SUMMER MONROE

"I love thongs because they make the ass look full and phat."

OBSSESSION

Photography by LRS Photography

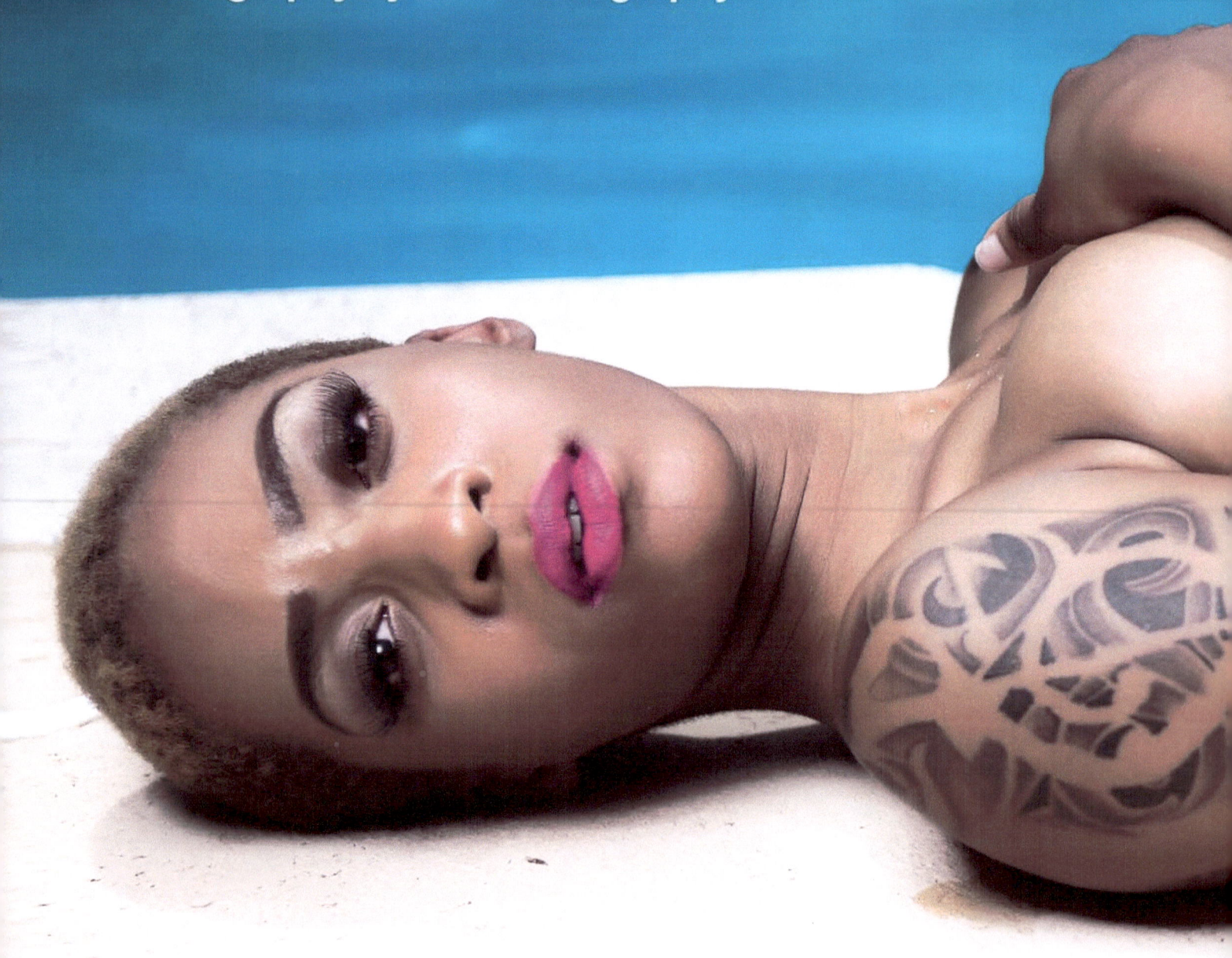

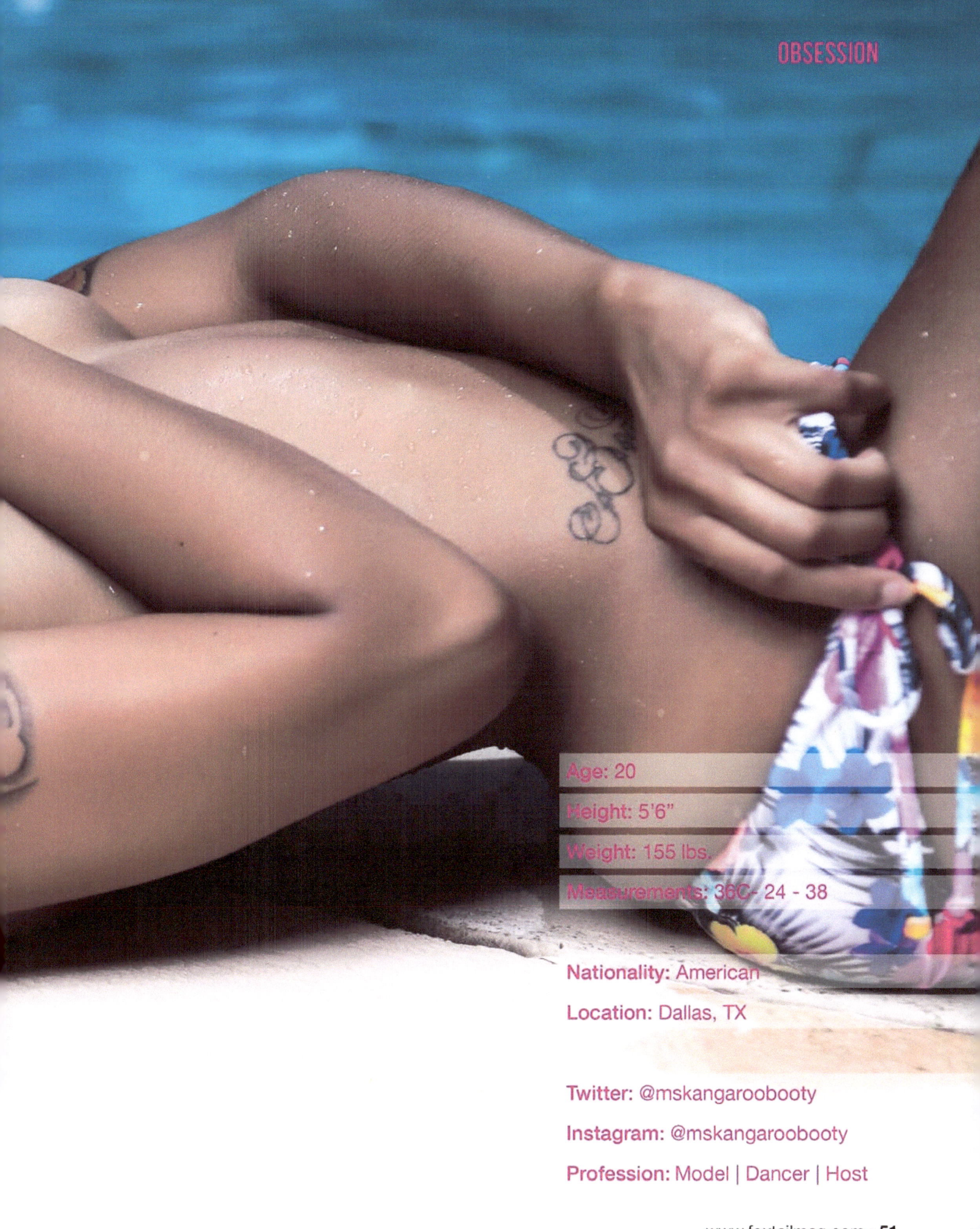

OBSESSION

Age: 20
Height: 5'6"
Weight: 155 lbs.
Measurements: 36C - 24 - 38

Nationality: American
Location: Dallas, TX

Twitter: @mskangaroobooty
Instagram: @mskangaroobooty
Profession: Model | Dancer | Host

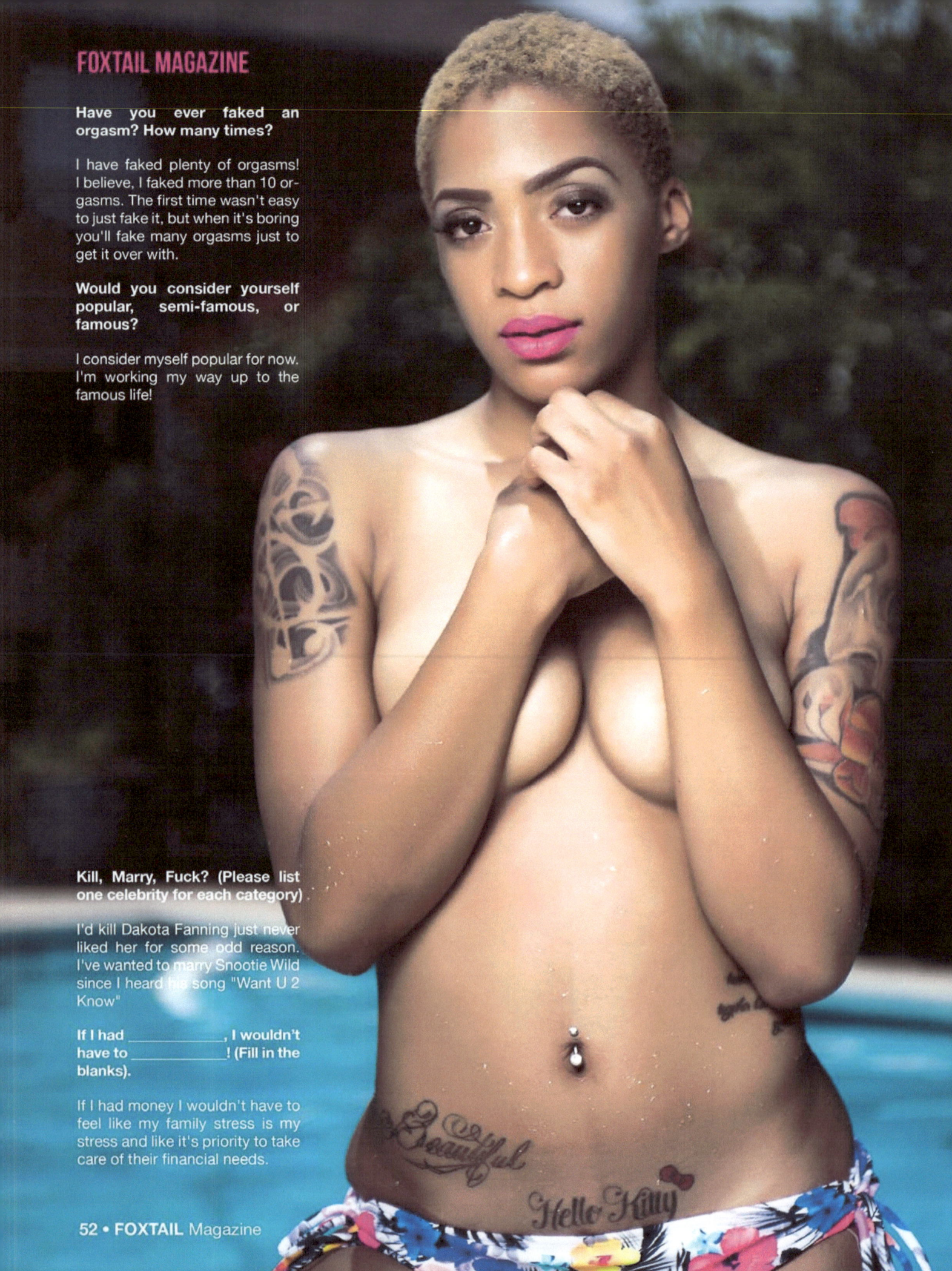

FOXTAIL MAGAZINE

Have you ever faked an orgasm? How many times?

I have faked plenty of orgasms! I believe, I faked more than 10 orgasms. The first time wasn't easy to just fake it, but when it's boring you'll fake many orgasms just to get it over with.

Would you consider yourself popular, semi-famous, or famous?

I consider myself popular for now. I'm working my way up to the famous life!

Kill, Marry, Fuck? (Please list one celebrity for each category)

I'd kill Dakota Fanning just never liked her for some odd reason. I've wanted to marry Snootie Wild since I heard his song "Want U 2 Know"

If I had _____, I wouldn't have to _____! (Fill in the blanks).

If I had money I wouldn't have to feel like my family stress is my stress and like it's priority to take care of their financial needs.

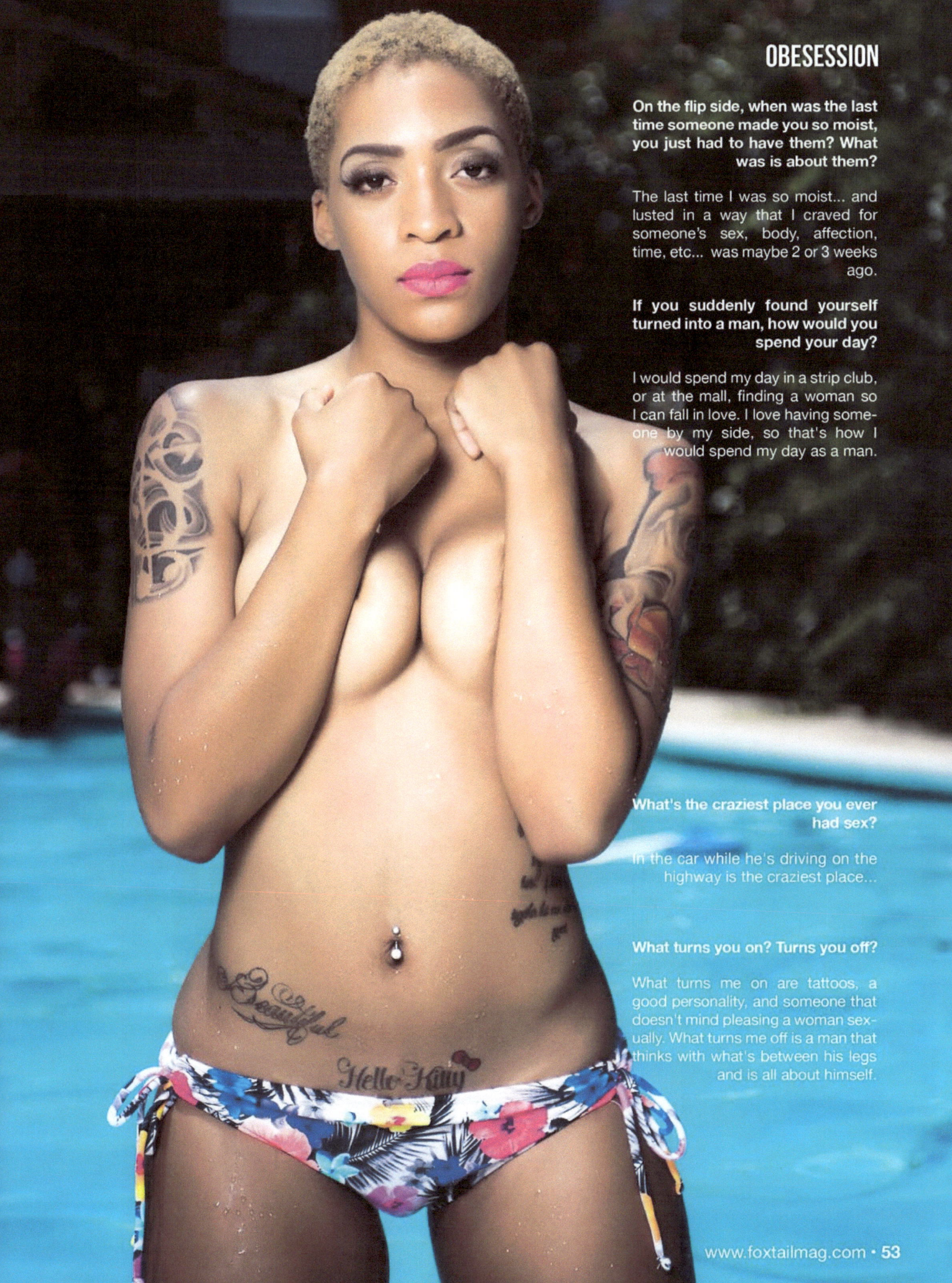

OBSESSION

On the flip side, when was the last time someone made you so moist, you just had to have them? What was is about them?

The last time I was so moist... and lusted in a way that I craved for someone's sex, body, affection, time, etc... was maybe 2 or 3 weeks ago.

If you suddenly found yourself turned into a man, how would you spend your day?

I would spend my day in a strip club, or at the mall, finding a woman so I can fall in love. I love having someone by my side, so that's how I would spend my day as a man.

What's the craziest place you ever had sex?

In the car while he's driving on the highway is the craziest place...

What turns you on? Turns you off?

What turns me on are tattoos, a good personality, and someone that doesn't mind pleasing a woman sexually. What turns me off is a man that thinks with what's between his legs and is all about himself.

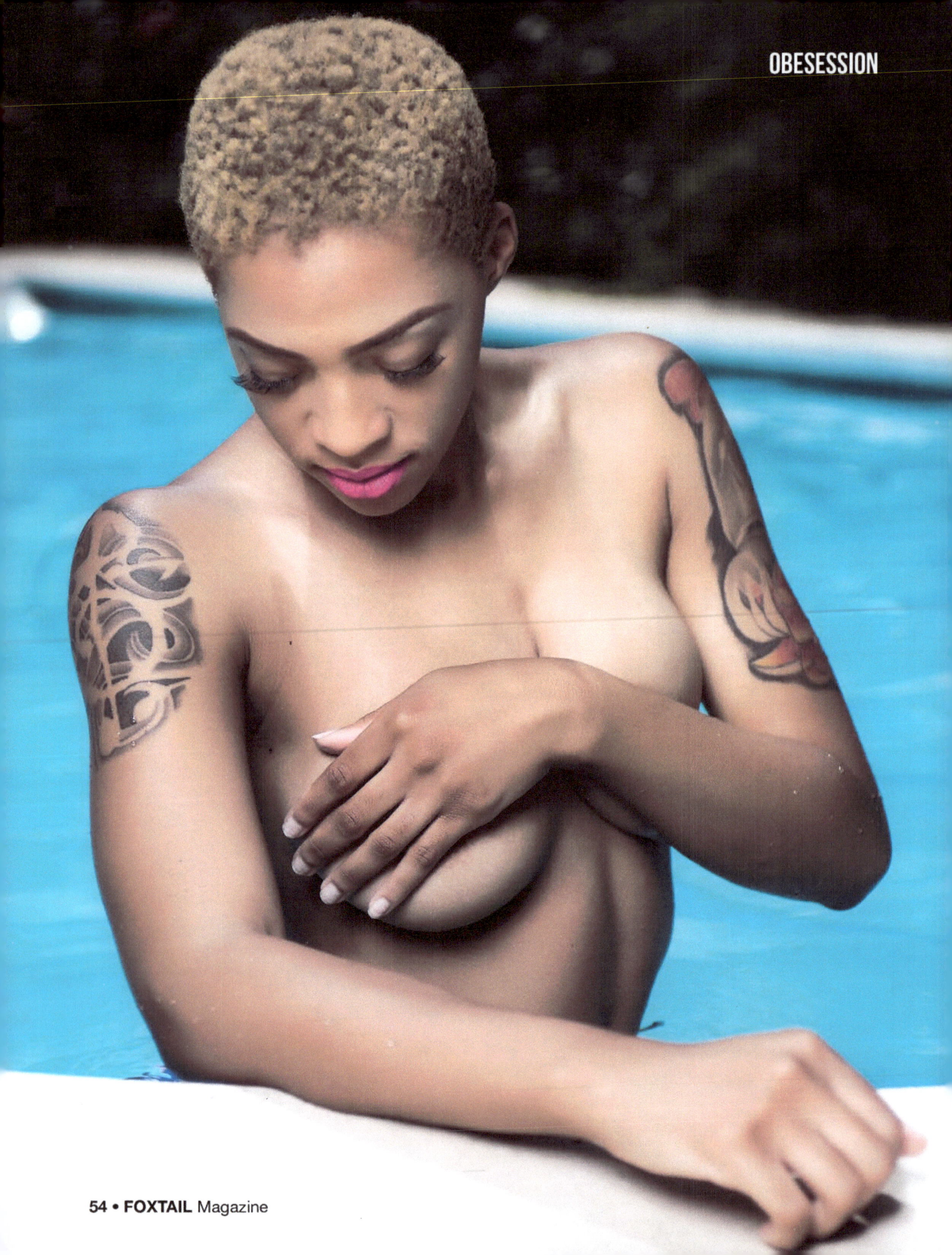